Dale Earnhardt
Always a Champion

A Tribute and Farewell to the Intimidator

TRIUMPH
B O O K S
CHICAGO

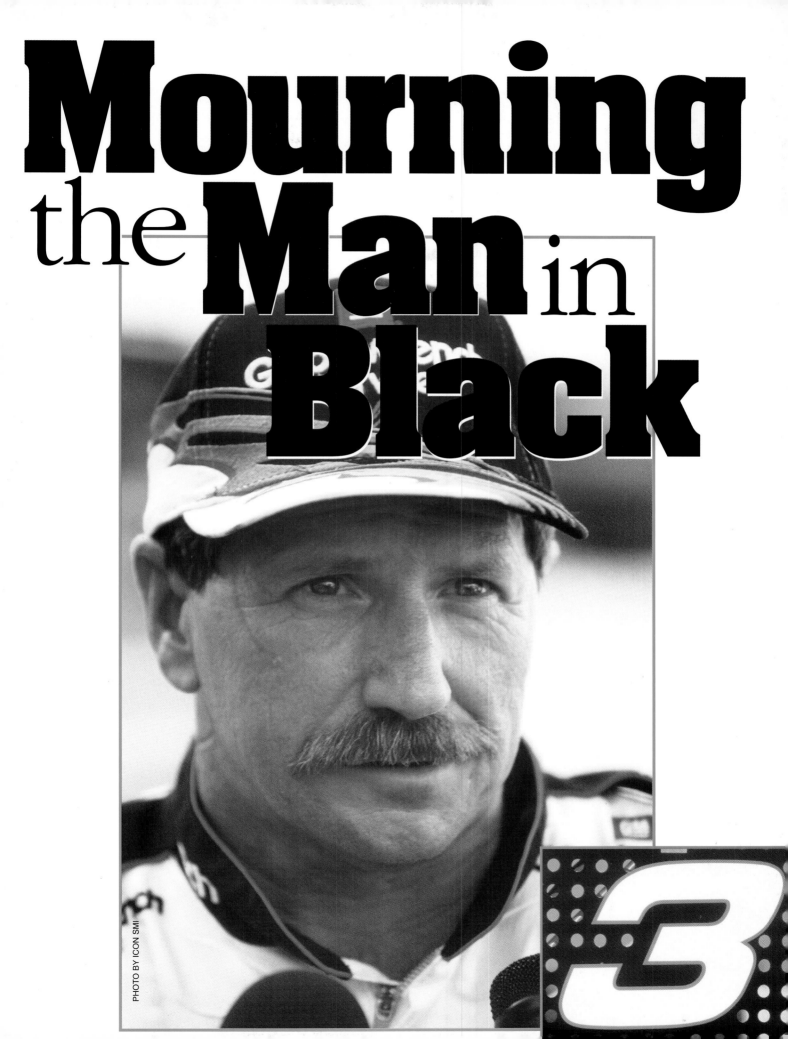

Mourning the Man in Black

Contents

Linc Wonham/Executive Editor

Ray Ramos/Creative Director

Aaron George, Tom Caestecker/Editors

Don Mastri, Gina Ruffolo/Graphic Designers

Contributors

Jeff Bartlett, David Fantle, Thomas Johnson, Benjamin Roberts, Jason Wilde/Feature Writers

Photos: AP/Wide World, Icon SMI, Timepix, Reuters, Driverona mission.com

The Final Turn

EARNHARDT FOUGHT TO THE END ON A TRAGIC DAY AT DAYTONA

By Jason Wilde

AP/WIDE WORLD PHOTOS

The Turn-4 crash ended Earnhardt's life just moments before the conclusion of his 22nd Daytona 500.

Seconds before the checkered flag on Sunday, February 18, less than half a mile from the finish line, Dale Earnhardt's familiar black No. 3 Chevrolet slammed into the concrete outside retaining wall in Turn 4 of Daytona International Speedway in Daytona Beach, Florida. Suddenly, in the final turn of the final lap of NASCAR's greatest race, the sport had lost one of its greatest legends.

And it will never be the same without him.

Earnhardt's fatal crash cast an enormous pall over what had been one of the most competitive Daytona 500s in the 43-year history of the Super Bowl of stock-car races.

Earnhardt, the driver who had come to define NASCAR, died instantly from massive head injuries.

"Incredible. Just incredible," driver Jeremy Mayfield said. "You figure he'll bounce right back. Your first thought is, 'Hey, he'll probably come back next week at Rockingham and beat us all.'"

That will not happen. The Intimidator is suddenly gone. Those left behind were stunned as word of his death spread. Fans cried, the large American flag in the middle of the speedway's infield was lowered to half-staff.

The Final Turn

Nearly two hours after the race, NASCAR president Mike Helton, his voice cracking with emotion, walked into the infield media center with the news everyone feared.

"This is undoubtedly one of the toughest announcements I have ever personally had to make," Helton said. "We've lost Dale Earnhardt."

Days before the race, Richard Childress, the owner of Earnhardt's Chevrolet, surveyed aerodynamics changes and new restrictions placed on cars by NASCAR and made a prediction. "It's going to be the best Daytona 500 we've ever seen," he said.

Instead, it was the saddest.

Earnhardt was the first driver killed in the Daytona 500, which began in 1959. Six drivers had died of injuries from wrecks during practice or qualifying races for the 500, but never in the race itself. Neil Bonnett, Earnhardt's best friend in racing, was killed in practice in 1994. Rodney Orr died in a wreck three days later, also in practice, and was the last Winston Cup driver killed at the track until Earnhardt's crash. ➜

His journey ended in a most noble way, as Earnhardt fought to secure the victory of team member Waltrip.

An empty victory

Michael Waltrip

Earnhardt was a seven-time Winston Cup champion, and his 76 victories were the most among active drivers. Earnhardt won more races at Daytona International Speedway — 32 — than any other NASCAR driver.

But he'd been the runner-up at the Daytona 500 four times the last eight years and it wasn't until 1998, in his 20th attempt, that he captured the most coveted checkered flag in stock-car racing. In the final race of his career, Earnhardt was credited with 12th place.

"He had what I felt were life-ending type injuries at the time of impact and nothing could be done for him," said Dr. Steve Bohannon, an emergency physician at Halifax Medical Center who also works for the speedway.

Michael Waltrip, the driver Earnhardt thought of as a younger brother, won the race, while his son, Dale Earnhardt Jr., finished second. It should have been the biggest moment in the short history of the Dale Earnhardt Inc. race team, a 1-2 finish at the Great American Race.

Waltrip, the younger brother of recently retired NASCAR star Darrell Waltrip, had spent his entire career struggling in the shadow of his brother, who won 84 races and three

championships. Then, at the end of last season, Earnhardt gave Michael the break he'd been waiting for, hiring him as a teammate of Earnhardt Jr. and Steve Park on the Dale Earnhardt Inc. team. Earnhardt himself, meanwhile, continued to drive cars owned by Childress, his longtime friend.

But for Waltrip, who had been winless during the previous 15 seasons and 462 races in his Winston Cup career, the monumental victory was rendered completely meaning-less. When he first reached Victory Lane, Waltrip was overjoyed, shouting, "This is the Daytona 500, and I won it! I won the Daytona 500! I can't believe it!"

But he was somber as it became apparent that his new boss, who gave him a chance to race with the best

equipment of his career, was badly injured.

"I'd rather be anywhere right now but here," said Waltrip, who took the lead 16 laps from the end of the 200-lap race. "The only reason I won this race was Dale Earnhardt."

Waltrip didn't learn until later that Earnhardt had died.

"He wasn't just my owner. He was my friend," Waltrip said. "My heart is hurting."

After Dale Jr. crossed the line 0.124 of a second behind Waltrip, he left his car on pit road and tried to get to the scene of his father's accident.

Although no one will ever know for sure, Earnhardt — known as a relentless and ruthless competitor on the track and a generous, unselfish man off it — died doing something so out of character that it could turn out to be his legacy in the sport he came to define.

Running third on the final lap, with one last chance to perhaps pass Waltrip and his son, Earnhardt chose instead to keep the rest of the field at arm's length, to let his son and the

Waltrip credited his teammate with the victory, saying, "The only reason I won this race was Dale Earnhardt."

newest driver on his team fight it out for the victory while he protected them from the contenders in pursuit. In fact, it appeared as if Earnhardt's focus was not on winning, as it had always been since his rookie season of 1979, but instead simply on preventing the other racers from intruding on "The Earnhardt Connection" 1-2-3 finish.

"It's ironic that people talk about how selfish Dale Earnhardt was on the racetrack. He was a winner and when he buckled that helmet on he was focused on winning. But those of us who knew him off the track know how unselfish he really was," said Dr. Jerry Punch, a TV commentator and close friend of Earnhardt.

That others-first attitude was on display as Earnhardt blocked contenders from advancing on his teammates,

rather than trying to win the race himself.

"The irony is that, for the first time on the track, you saw him be very unselfish in the final laps," Punch said. "In my opinion, he had a car that could have made a move. He could have pulled up in front of Sterling Marlin and maybe Kenny Schrader, probably drafted by and won his second Daytona 500. [Instead], Dale Earnhardt lost his life trying to secure a win for his friend, Michael Waltrip.

"What Dale Earnhardt did in those final laps is what a father would do for a son, who was running right in front of him, or a brother would do for a brother," Punch added. "And Michael Waltrip was like a little brother he never had. [Earnhardt] stayed in the third spot and ran a 180 mph screen. He kept Marlin and Schrader, and the others who didn't have a chance coming down the stretch, behind him so that his son and his friend could have an opportunity to win.

"It was a very unselfish move and one that many of us who have known him for years understood." ➔

The Final Turn

No signs of life

The crash began when the back left corner of Earnhardt's famed black No. 3 Chevrolet bumped with Sterling Marlin's Dodge. Earnhardt's car fishtailed slightly and briefly slid to its left, down toward the infield, before suddenly swinging back to the right and cutting across traffic at a sharp angle. His car hit the wall headfirst and Ken Schrader's yellow Pontiac crashed into the passenger side.

With Earnhardt's Chevy already smoking at the front, Schrader's car stayed lodged into its side, forming a T. The cars careened again off the wall, plowing into the final turn and sliding to a stop on the infield grass.

Schrader climbed out of his car and ran to check on Earnhardt. He immediately waved for emergency workers to come help.

"I guess someone got into Dale because Dale got into me and then we went up," said Schrader, who was not injured. "We hit pretty hard, and Dale hit harder."

When emergency workers arrived at the accident scene, Earnhardt was not breathing, had no pulse and had blood in his ears and throat. The first member of the track medical team to reach the car clamped an oxygen mask on Earnhardt and realized he was already too late.

Those close to him, including Dale Earnhardt Jr. (left), were devastated by the loss of a friend and racing legend.

Resuscitation efforts began while he was still in his car, with the first paramedic applying the oxygen mask from the right side window while through the driver's-side window another doctor was administering CPR and a second paramedic held Earnhardt's head. At the same time, firefighters were working to cut the roof off the car to try to facilitate Earnhardt's removal.

"That took about five or 10 minutes, during which time we did CPR," Bohannon said. "When the roof came off, Dr. [Alfred] Alson and I both dentified this was a very bad situation, a 'load-and-go' situation."

Transport to the hospital took less than two minutes, and resuscitation efforts continued during the trip, Bohannon said. A trauma team including a neurosurgeon and several other doctors was waiting when Earnhardt arrived at 4:54 p.m. at the hospital, where he was "placed on a ventilator, multiple IV lines were given, IV fluids, chest tubes, various diagnostic tests," Bohannon said.

"We all did everything we could for him," Bohannon said. "He never showed any signs of life."

Earnhardt was pronounced dead at 5:16 p.m. Eastern Standard Time, 22 minutes after he arrived at the hospital. His wife, Teresa, was at his side. ➔

Costly changes

A dull race the previous year prompted NASCAR to alter the rules and equipment for this Daytona 500. The goal was to slow down the cars and make them run closer together, to produce the kind of tight, thrilling racing that fans love and many drivers hate. Due in large part to those aerodynamic changes, the race produced 49 lead changes among 14 drivers. Last year, there were just nine lead changes and hardly any intense racing.

Insiders said no one was more pleased by the return of old-time racing than Earnhardt, who was considered to be the best and most fearless driver in NASCAR when it came to snaking his way through a pack of speeding cars separated only by inches. No one figured to thrive in such an environment more than Earnhardt.

Instead, Earnhardt's death is the fourth in NASCAR since the start of the 2000 season. Busch Series driver Adam Petty, grandson of seven-time champion Richard Petty, died in May at New Hampshire International Speedway. Winston Cup competitor Kenny Irwin was killed at the same track in July, and Craftsman Truck Series driver Tony Roper died at Texas Motor Speedway in Fort Worth in October.

All three died of the same injury that presumably killed Earnhardt. The fracture is caused when a driver's car decelerates quickly but his head and helmet continue to move forward, causing stress to the neck.

Earnhardt wore an old-fashioned, open-faced helmet and chose not to use some of NASCAR's other basic safety innovations. He refused to wear a Head And Neck Safety (HANS)

brace that recently has been touted as a way to help prevent serious head injuries.

Bohannon doubted that a full-face helmet or the HANS device would have saved his life.

"I know the full-face helmet wouldn't have made any difference whatsoever. He had no evidence of facial injuries," Bohannon said. "I don't know if the HANS device would have helped. I suspect not."

Only about one in 10 drivers wore the HANS device Sunday. Those who don't wear it have said it was too uncomfortable and limited their mobility.

"It's difficult to talk about safety devices when we're talking about the loss of someone we cared about so much," Punch said. "The HANS device is a good one. But, even as safe as these cars are, I'm not sure the HANS device would have made

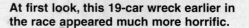

At first look, this 19-car wreck earlier in the race appeared much more horrific.

that much difference with the massive deceleration Dale Earnhardt experienced at 185 mph. Typically in these cases, the driver sustains a fracture to the head. That is not a survivable injury.

"The injuries that are most survivable look the worst," Punch continued. "The violent tumbles dissipate energy slowly and result mostly in broken bones and maybe a concussion. But the ones like Sunday, where the car veers suddenly into the wall, are the worst."

The crash, however, didn't look that serious at first. Most of the fans' attention at the time was on the fight for the checkered flag between Waltrip and Earnhardt Jr. In fact, with two- and three-wide racing and constantly changing positions, there was a far more dangerous-looking wreck 26 laps earlier. The 19-car accident sent Tony Stewart's Pontiac flying through the air and over the roof of another car. Stewart also was taken to the hospital, where he was treated

for a concussion. Earnhardt's crash, meanwhile, was deadly. Two months shy of his 50th birthday, on the final turn of the final lap of his 676th Winston Cup race and his 22nd Daytona 500, The Intimidator lost his life.

And the sport will never be the same without him. ∎

King of the Road

of the

IN RACING AND IN LIFE, NOBODY DID IT QUITE LIKE EARNHARDT

By David Fantle and Thomas Johnson

Dale Earnhardt knew the risks. Despite being the first driver killed in the Daytona 500, he was well aware that six of his racing brethren had died of injuries from wrecks in qualifying races for the 500. For all of his 49 years, Earnhardt lived life in the fast lane. The Intimidator, as they called him for his fierce, competitive style, was still at the top of his game, and he bristled when some suggested he permanently park his famous black No. 3 Chevrolet and let the younger guys take over.

For all of his 49 years, Earnhardt lived life in the fast lane.

King of the Road

"If physically and mentally I can't do this, [I'll retire]. If I can't go down in the corner and drive competitively with the next guy and beat him or win a race, that's going to [determine when I stop]," Earnhardt said last year. "Your reflexes and health or whatever is going to tell on you. I don't see it happening in the next three years."

The competitive juices ran in Earnhardt from the start. And he never stopped putting the pedal to the metal. It was high gear or nothing.

A racing family

Dale Earnhardt was born April 29, 1951, in Kannapolis, North Carolina. Although young Earnhardt helped his parents work on the family farm, it was in his pedigree to pursue a career behind the wheel of his race car. Although never a NASCAR Winston Cup series champion, his father, Ralph, was an accomplished driver in his own right. A household name at North Carolina short tracks, the elder

Earnhardt ran up some decent numbers during a 23-year racing career. He won NASCAR's Sportsman Division championship in 1956 and in 1961 posted seven top-10 finishes in eight starts in the Winston Cup series division — good for 17th in the standings. Ralph Earnhardt was inducted in the National Motorsports Press Association's Hall of Fame at Darlington, South Carolina Raceway, as well as the International Motorsports Hall of Fame in Talladega, Alabama.

While Ralph was off racing, Martha Earnhardt, the matriarch of the family, would stay home in Kannapolis and watch over their five children. "One time Ralph had went to Daytona one year and I didn't go," she said. "I was home with the kids, Dale, Randy and Danny, and they were just trying my nerves to see how bad they could really upset me. I just grabbed a belt and started swinging, I didn't care who I was going to hit. Dale hollered at Randy

and Danny and said, 'Boys, y'all run. Mom's gone crazy!' "

It was through his father that Earnhardt learned to love and respect the sport of car racing. A high school dropout, Earnhardt began racing Hobby-class cars at local events while still a teenager. He worked full-time during the day, welding and mounting tires, and either racing or tinkering with his cars at night. He used his meager wages to buy parts, sometimes even borrowing money with the hopes of paying back the bank on Monday, after a weekend of racing.

Tragically, his father would never see his son attain international fame. On Sept. 26, 1973, Ralph Earnhardt died of a heart attack at the age of 45, ironically while working on his race car. The tragedy hit Dale Earnhardt hard and gave him a renewed determination to dedicate his life to race-car driving. Earnhardt continued to compete on the Sportsman circuit, racing →

Although never a NASCAR Winston Cup series champion, his father, Ralph, was an accomplished driver in his own right.

With legions of fans everywhere he traveled, Earnhardt was one of most legendary figures in the history of stock-car racing.

King of the Road

Career man

Earnhardt made his Winston Cup debut in 1975 in the World 600 at Charlotte Motor Speedway, finishing 22nd in a Dodge owned by Ed Negre, right behind Richard Childress. For his part, Earnhardt earned $2,245. During the next three years, Earnhardt made only eight more starts, ending with the Dixie 500 in Atlanta in 1978. Earnhardt, driving a second car for Rod Osterlund, finished a respectable fourth, one spot behind Osterlund's regular driver Dave Marcis.

This race would prove to be Earnhardt's biggest career break. Marcis left the Osterlund team to form his own. This left an opening and Osterlund, after considering several candidates, tapped Earnhardt to be his driver for the 1979 Winston Cup season. ➔

at local speedways such as Hickory, Concord and the Metrolina Fairgrounds.

According to Martha Earnhardt, her lifelong exposure to racing through her husband, son and now grandson, is often nerve-racking. "I think it gets worse instead of better," she said. "When you get older, your nerves are not quite as strong.

When Ralph started I was only about 19 years old and I really didn't have sense enough to worry.

"When Dale got in a race car, that was just altogether different from Ralph," she continued. "I grew up with Ralph racing and I knew he knew what he was doing. When Dale got in, that was part of me getting in that car and it was just a different story."

Dale Earn

1975 - Made stock-car racing debut on May 25, finishing 22nd in the World 600 at Charlotte Motor Speedway.

1979 - Earned first victory on April 1 at Bristol, Tenn.; Won Rookie of the Year Award.

1980 - Won first Winston Cup Championship, becoming only driver to win Rookie of the Year and season championship back-to-back.

1986 - Won five races to take second Winston Cup Championship.

1987 - Won 11 races for third Winston Cup Championship, finishing in top five 21 times in 29 races.

hardt Career Highlights

1990 - Won nine times to take fourth Winston Cup Championship, earning a then-record $3,083,056.

1991 - Won four races for fifth Winston Cup Championship.

1993 - Won six races to earn sixth Winston Cup Championship.

1994 - Won seventh Winston Cup Championship, tying Richard Petty for most career titles. Topped $3-million mark in earnings for third time in five years.

1996 - Became third driver to start 500 consecutive Winston Cup races.

1997 - Became first driver to reach $30 million in American Motor Sports winnings and first race car driver to appear on box of Wheaties Cereal.

1998 - Won first Daytona 500 in 20th career start, breaking a 59-race winless streak overall. Finished eighth in season standings, his 18th top-10 finish in 20 years.

1999 - Won 10th consecutive Twin 125 qualifying race at Daytona.

2000 - Won Winston 500 on Oct. 15 at Talladega Superspeedway for final career victory.

Career Pole Positions: 22.
Career top 5 finishes: 268.
Career top 10 finishes: 404.

Winston Cup Championships: 7
(1980, 1986, 1987, 1990, 1991, 1993, 1994)

IROC Championships: 3
(1990, 1995, 1999)

American Driver of the Year: 2 (1987, 1994)

Won record nine races at Talladega Superspeedway.

Owns record 34 victories in all forms of racing at Daytona Speedway.

King of the Road

In his inaugural season, Earnhardt took home the rookie title, besting Harry Grant, Terry Labonte and Joe Millikan. This came after Earnhardt scored his first Winston Cup win in just his 16th start, and finished the season with 11 top-five finishes.

Earnhardt continued his impressive record during his sophomore year on the circuit, edging out racing legend Cale Yarborough to win the 1980 NASCAR Winston Cup championship, the first of what would become a regular feat. In the process, Earnhardt became the only driver to win the rookie and championship honors in consecutive years.

Midway through Earnhardt's rookie season, Osterlund sold his team to Jim Stacy. Earnhardt, after competing in just four races, joined forces with Childress, completing the season as a member of his team. Beginning with the 1982 season, Earnhardt competed for Bud Moore and big-buck sponsor Wrangler for two seasons, winning three races and finishing as high as eighth in the overall point standings driving in the number-15 Fords. In an April 1982 race, Earnhardt fractured a knee in a crash at Talladega, but didn't miss a race.

The right stuff

Meanwhile, Childress, with driver Ricky Rudd, was building his team into a powerhouse contender. Earnhardt returned to the Childress team as the 1984 season began. It was a marriage made in racing heaven. After just two years of competition, Earnhardt won the 1986 Winston Cup championship.

In 1986, Earnhardt began cementing his legendary status on the racetrack, collecting six more Winston Cup championships over a nine-season period, tying Richard Petty for the most championships (seven) in a single career. Together, Earnhardt and Childress won championships in 1986, '87, '90, '91, '93 and '94. He finished second in the standings to Bobby Labonte last year and was determined to make a run for a record eighth championship in the 2001 season.

In 1990, Earnhardt earned a then-record $3 million in prize money. His career winnings exceeded $41 million.

Daytona at last

In February 1998, Earnhardt was named to the list of NASCAR's 50 greatest drivers as the sport marked its 50th anniversary, joining his late father on that list. That same year he finally won the Daytona 500, setting off a memorable celebration that included him spinning his car across the grass in the track's trioval.

While it seemed that Earnhardt had racked up wins in every major NASCAR racing event, one title that had eluded him was the Daytona 500. In what would be the capping of an illustrious career, Earnhardt won the 1998 race, the 71st win of his career in 575 races. This would come after his 20th attempt at Daytona. ➔

In 1990, Earnhardt earned a then-record $3 million in prize money. His career winnings exceeded $41 million.

NASCAR
WINSTON CUP SERIES
CHAMPION

PHOENIX INTERNATIONAL RACEWAY

NOVEMBER 1990
PHOENIX INTERNATIONAL RACEWAY

Earnhardt hoists his trophy after winning the 1990 Checker 500 at Phoenix International Raceway.

CHECKER 500 Racing Team

GOODYEAR

GoodWrench

76

Dale Earnhardt

AC

King of the Road

The long-awaited victory was emotional and sweet for Earnhardt. "Yes! Yes! Yes!," he exalted after the win. "Twenty years! Can you believe it!"

Although he won the Daytona 500 only once (1998), Earnhardt was Daytona's all-time leader with 34 victories at the storied track. About his 500 win, Earnhardt said: "This win is for all of our fans and all the people who told me, 'Dale, this is your year.' There was a lot of hard work that went into this and I have to thank every member of the Richard Childress Racing team. I have had a lot of great fans and people behind me all through the years and I just can't thank them enough ... The Daytona 500 is over. And we won it! We won it!"

After the Daytona win, the most popular and charismatic figure in stock-car racing history went on the talk-show circuit, even appearing on "Late Night With David Letterman." There he good-naturedly read "Dale Earnhardt's Top 10 Reasons It Took Me 20 Years To Win The Daytona 500." Among the reasons:

- It took me 19 years to realize I had the emergency brake on.
- Finally rotated and balanced my mustache. ➜

Earnhardt embraces daughter Nicole at the 1991 Busch Clash.

On top of his game to the bitter end

The common sense in all of us tries to tell us that Dale Earnhardt Sr. never should have gone down this way, with his car becoming his coffin on the last lap of the Daytona 500.

The sensible side says that a 49-year old man should've given up his seat in the cockpit of a race car going nearly 200 miles per hour. Or at least he should've announced his retirement, backed off the pedal and rode around on a nice farewell tour.

Earnhardt, however, was not a common driver, and the words 'back off' did not evolve in his vocabulary. He had no reason to back off. Age should not be the maxim by which retirement is measured. Ability should be that yardstick, and if we're measuring it that way then Earnhardt was nowhere near the rocking chair.

He had ability and he had a goal: to win his eighth Winston Cup championship and break the tie of seven titles he shared with fellow NASCAR legend Richard Petty.

Earnhardt's driving skills had not eroded anywhere close to the point that he was a detriment to other drivers. He was a detriment to the other drivers because he could still outrun them, still battle them side-by-side through a turn and still plant them into a wall if he deemed it appropriate.

Earnhardt still had plenty left, evidenced by last year's second-place finish in the NASCAR Winston Cup standings. You don't put a thoroughbred out to pasture in his prime, and you don't take away a driver's wheel when he's still capable of winning.

In fact, Earnhardt was still so good and so tough that it made his death in a racing crash almost inconceivable.

The common-sense side of us wishes Earnhardt had walked away a little sooner and lived to watch his son become a Winston Cup champion. But Earnhardt was an uncommon driver and an uncommon competitor. You can't ask someone of that caliber to walk away at the top of his craft. Earnhardt might never have walked away, so perhaps he went down in the most appropriate way possible. He was in a race car, unselfishly paving the way for his son to possibly win the Daytona 500, and because of that he died with uncommon valor.

That is how most drivers would like to be remembered, and how most will remember Earnhardt.

"I've told my wife many times, 'If anything ever happens to me in a race car, you just remember it was exactly what I was wanting to do,' " said Winston Cup veteran Mike Wallace. "The only thing I can say is it's what Dale Earnhardt wanted to do. He died doing what he loved to do."

How many of us in life get to go out that way?

— By Jeff Bartlett, NASCAR writer
for Checkered Flag magazine.

King of the Road

- My new pit crew — The Spice Girls.
- This year, whenever I'd pass somebody, I'd give 'em the finger.

The legend grows

After the Daytona win, Earnhardt's legend grew, and so did the demand for his services.

In May 1998, Earnhardt made a guest voice appearance as himself on the animated FOX series, "King of the Hill."

"I had a great time working with the people from 'King of the Hill,'" Earnhardt said. "It was a surprise when they asked if I was interested in doing a part for the show. After talking to the writers I found out they are big NASCAR fans and they followed the series."

That same year he made a cameo appearance in the feature film *BASEketball*. In his screen debut, Earnhardt played a washed-up racecar driver who drives a taxi cab for a living.

"It was fun," Earnhardt said of his acting stint. "When we first arrived on the set, the crew stopped what they were doing and started applauding and congratulating me on the win. I guess they all got together on Sunday and watched the race. It was very flattering."

A beaming mother, Martha Earnhardt said, "I'm proud Dale has got to do what he has always wanted to do, and has really done well at it. He has been able to come as far and accomplish what he has, and I am just proud of him as a person, the person he has become.

"It's really amazing when you go to the grocery store and there's your kid's picture on a cereal box or a Sun-drop bottle, or you see him on a billboard on the side of the road. It's really hard to realize that's really your child."

Sixth on NASCAR's all-time win list with 76 victories, Earnhardt was enjoying a late-career resurgence. He finished second in the 2000 points standings to Bobby Labonte, a remarkable feat at his age.

In 1999, Earnhardt underwent back surgery for what doctors called an "anterior cervical discectomy and fusion (or ruptured disc in his spinal column)." The operation was considered a success and Earnhardt stayed out of his car for about six weeks, the longest absence of his storied career.

After the surgery Earnhardt returned with a vengeance in 2000. With a diversified business portfolio that included ownership of three Winston Cup teams for son Dale Earnhardt Jr., Steve Park and Michael Waltrip, as well as part-time operation for oldest son Kerry Earnhardt, his desire to get behind the wheel and compete never waned.

The year 2000 saw the 49-year-old racer again in the thick of the hunt for his eighth Winston Cup championship. Earnhardt's final career victory came on October 15 of last season at Talladega, Alabama, on the day Tony Roper ➜

Sixth on NASCAR's all-time win list with 76 victories, Earnhardt was enjoying a late-career resurgence.

All was well after this triumph at the 1995 Brickyard 400.

King of the Road

died from injuries he'd suffered in a Truck series crash at Texas Motor Speedway the night before.

It was a turnaround year for Earnhardt who was almost written off after going winless in 1997. The 1998 Daytona 500 win was to be his only victory that season. Still the veteran racer would hear nothing of retirement.

"I've got four years of racing left, at least," he said last summer. "Who knows? I might even drive another car with my own team. I'm not ruling anything out. I've got a job and an opportunity to win that eighth championship. That's what we're focusing on. That's what we're driving for. That's what we're working for.

"We're doing it with a more solid team than I've had in past years," he added. "I may have been hurt for the last two years and working with pain and stuff and didn't realize it until it got worse and worse. I had to have something to do about it. That's all in the past. It's over. We're healthy. The team is healthy."

Hands-on

Because of his tenacity and fierce competitive nature, Earnhardt was considered by race fans as either the most hated or most loved driver in NASCAR. About his manic schedule, fellow racing Hall-of-Famer Buddy Baker said jokingly, "I guess that's the price you pay to make $40 million."

For his part, Earnhardt fessed up to his workaholic tendencies. "I'm the kind of guy, I want to know everything," he said. "I want to know if there's an unhappy employee somewhere. I want to know what the balance is at the end of the day. If I know what's going on, then I can help in some way or control it."

Earnhardt's wife, Teresa, is also heavily involved in the business, handling several duties for the 300-employee corporation. The company is located on 350 acres of rolling farmland in the north Charlotte suburbs. It's housed in four buildings occupying more than 200,000 square feet, including the 108,000 square-foot main building.

Late last year, Earnhardt became part owner of a baseball team in the South Atlantic League, the Piedmont Boll Weevils, who changed their affiliation to the Chicago White Sox for this season. The franchise also changed its name to the driver's nickname, becoming the Kannapolis Intimidators.

But Earnhardt was more than just the weathered-looking and imposing mustachioed man behind the dark glasses. Said *The Charlotte Observer*. "He was a businessman who owned race teams and chicken farms. He was a genius for marketing his 'Intimidator' image, which sold a lot of T-shirts while also allowing him to carve out at least a small piece of privacy for him and his family." →

Earnhardt was considered by race fans as either the most hated or most loved driver in NASCAR.

King of the
Road

Earnhardt's popularity was chiefly responsible for enabling the sport's evolution from a regional pastime in the Southeast to a billion-dollar industry on the national stage. In fact, FOX only recently began airing NASCAR events to high viewership ratings. Fox's coverage of the 2001 Daytona 500 race earned an 8.4 rating and 19 share, the highest overnight rating for the race since 1986.

Stock-car racing has been rapidly growing in popularity, and Earnhardt is largely responsible. "Nobody has had more to do with that than No. 3," said *The Charlotte Observer*. "Dale Earnhardt was the embodiment of stock-car racing. He was its most honest image. He was dark speed, an Elvis smile, a blithe spirit who knew that racing was just that, racing, and really all the rules you needed were to race like a man and keep the pedal on the floor."

"Dale Earnhardt was the greatest race-car driver that ever lived," Ned Jarrett, a former NASCAR champion himself, told the Associated Press. "He could do things with a race car that no one else could."

The Intimidator to the end

As recently as last year, Earnhardt spoke about the sport that he loved as if he was just beginning his legendary career. "I'd like to win 25 more races before I quit racing," he said, "and I'd like to win another championship. That's on my list of things to do."

A racing purist, Earnhardt at times was critical of NASCAR for rules that he said were designed to slow drivers down. He preferred the 1980s when he and fellow drivers Darrell Waltrip and Rusty Wallace did a lot of "gouging and sticking." Today's racers, said Earnhardt, ride in a pack — "existing on the track together" — waiting for the perfect moment to

make the one move that could win the race. Ironically, at the 2001 Daytona 500, it was Earnhardt who may have exacted those rules in order to preserve the victory during the final lap of the race won by Michael Waltrip, driving a car Earnhardt owned.

"It's like having the privilege to race to win," Earnhardt said. "Guys play in the minor leagues and never get to go to the majors. Guys get to race in Busch or the truck series and never get an opportunity to drive a Cup car. I'm there. I have the opportunity. I'm excited about what I do. I'm not content with not winning. If somebody tells you I'm riding my years out, they're not paying attention."

The racing world never stopped paying attention to Dale Earnhardt. In addition to his mother, Martha, Earnhardt is survived by his wife, Teresa; two sons, Dale Jr., 27 and Kerry, 32, and two daughters, Kelly, 29 and Taylor Nicole, 13. ■

As recently as last year, Earnhardt spoke about the sport that he loved as if he was just beginning his legendary career.

The Intimi

dator

THE ONE-OF-A-KIND EARNHARDT MORE THAN LIVED UP TO HIS NICKNAME

By James Raia

More than flat tires, oil leaks or blown transmissions, Dale Earnhardt gave his fellow NASCAR drivers their biggest concern — intimidation.

"There is no worse sight than seeing Dale Earnhardt in your rear-view mirror with one lap left," was the refrain repeated for more than two decades by veteran and rookie drivers alike.

It helped Earnhardt earn the nickname of "The Intimidator," a moniker that defined the driver's aggressive and fearless racing style throughout his 76 career wins and 676 career Winston Cup events.

When he crashed and died in the final yards of the 2001 Daytona 500, Earnhardt was competing in his 648th consecutive event — seven starts shy of Terry Labonte's record. His car was recorded with a 12th-place finish, a fatal, eerie start and end to what Earnhardt had hoped would lead to a record-setting eighth season championship. ➜

Old habits die hard

There wasn't much of a clue of Earnhardt's future racing prowess when he made his NASCAR debut in May 1975 in the World 600 at Charlotte Motor Speedway. He started in 33rd position and finished 22nd, some 45 laps behind winner Richard Petty.

But in April 1979 at Bristol, Tennessee, Earnhardt's cavalcade of career victories began. And so did his legacy as a tough-as-nails competitor.

Skilled, brash and savvy, he tried maneuvering into openings on race tracks observers said other drivers couldn't even see. And just like country singer Johnny Cash, Earnhardt's image was enhanced by his trademark black attire and strong opinions. In addition to "The Intimidator," others called him "Ironhead" or "The Man in Black."

Regardless of what he was called, Earnhardt was a man of hard-to-break traditions. He proudly wore his black jeans, black shirt and trademark thick mustache. He also preferred to wear an open-face helmet while driving. Many of his colleagues had switched to the more safety-conscious, full-face helmets, but Earnhardt said he could see better in the traditional helmet.

He drove a black race car, No. 3. The combined color and number became so popular, race fans simply put black "3" decals on their cars. Words weren't required.

Even *The Charlotte Observer* editorial cartoonist used the black 3 to honor Earnhardt. In the edition printed the day following the driver's death, the newspaper ran a three-panel cartoon. The first panel was a black 3, the second a 3 sprouting racing wings and in the third, the 3 had transformed into just the race wings.

Whether using his icy stare or rough tactics, Earnhardt was the master of intimidation.

Again, words weren't necessary.

In the 21-year span of racing since he claimed his first title until his final win on October 15 last year at Talladega, Alabama, Earnhardt won at least one race in 19 seasons. He won two races or more in 15 seasons, including the first of his seven Winston Cup titles in 1980 when he claimed five races.

Earnhardt won 11 times in 29 starts in 1987 and nine times in 29 starts in 1990. He compiled 281 top-five and 428 top-10 finishes in his career. Last season, he competed in 35 events, the most season starts in his career. With the half-century age

plateau approaching, Earnhardt still won twice.

In recent years, when NASCAR safety innovations were introduced, Earnhardt dismissed them, including his refusal to wear the HANS (Head And Neck Safety) brace recently introduced as a way to help prevent serious head injuries. Earnhardt also preferred to use a low-back seat, long after competitors had switched to high-back seats.

When restrictor carburetor plates were ordered by NASCAR last season to slow speed and hopefully have drivers run closer together, Earnhardt bawked. "A race driver hates a

restrictor plate," he said. "I think the same thing I've always thought about restrictor plates. It's not racing. Racing is going out there and trying to be the fastest guy on the track."

Earnhardt followed the racing roots of his father Ralph, a well-known competitor at short-track circuits throughout the Carolinas. As a boy, he watched his father build engines and cars. And when his father died of a heart attack when Earnhardt was in his 20s, he knew what his future held. "When he passed away, Earnhardt explained in a 1999 interview with *The Washington Post*, "I felt like, 'I have to do this. I've got to do this.'" ➜

Earnhardt shunned some of the safety features utilized by his peers, such as the HANS (Head And Neck Safety) brace.

The Intimidator

Building a reputation

After four years of only a combined handful of Winston Cup races, Earnhardt got his first victory in 1979 in his first full season. The win propelled him to Winston Cup rookie of the year honors. He followed in 1980 with his initial season championship.

Through the 1980s, Earnhardt's driving style continued to give further credence to his moniker. Fellow drivers and race fans knew Earnhardt as gruff, stubborn and arrogant — all traits that suited his aggressive racing ways and made him his sport's most controversial and respected driver.

Earnhardt was perhaps best known for maneuvering his way through tight packs of cars that were often separated by inches. Some drivers said he was so skilled at drafting — the process of using the slipstream of an opponent's car to your own advantage — that friend and fellow-champion Dale Jarrett once said he believed Earnhardt could "see the air."

Earnhardt also had his detractors. He was often booed as much as he was cheered by some fans. There were many race followers who felt Earnhardt was a bully and drove to his wins by risking his own safety and the safety of others by purposely knocking others out of races. Still, none of his competitors questioned Earnhardt's skills.

"NASCAR lost its greatest driver and probably the greatest driver it will ever have," said fellow competitor Johnny Benson. "Our sport will go on, but I don't think it will ever be the same."

Beyond his uncanny ability to get to the front of the pack, it was his wont to remain there that highlighted much of Earnhardt's career.

During the 1980s, it seemed nearly every week he was involved ➜

The Intimidator waged some of his fiercest battles with Gordon and his colorful DuPont-sponsored car.

Though an intimidator behind the wheel,
Earnhardt was gracious to his many supporters.

in fender-bumping battles with his top competitors, not the least of whom were Geoff Bodine, Darrell Waltrip and Bill Elliott.

Among fans and his peers, Earnhardt had a reputation as a driver who would take chances others wouldn't. At the Atlanta Motor Speedway, for instance, he would pass drivers using an outside groove, an almost unheard-of strategy.

In 1992, at the International Race of Champions (IROC) in Charlotte, he somehow shot from third to win the race in the final few hundred yards. The following year, he won four consecutive Winston Cup races, becoming the third modern-era driver to win four straight events.

Another example of Earnhardt's brash racing approach occurred in 1995 at Bristol Motor Speedway. Early in a race on the high-banked, half-mile oval, NASCAR officials relegated Earnhardt to the back of the field for knocking Rusty Wallace into a wall. Earnhardt had also collided with Derrick Cope and Lake Speed, leaving his car badly battered.

Despite his car's demolition-derby appearance, Earnhardt was in second place on the final turn. He rammed into race leader and eventual winner Labonte as the duo approached the finish line. Earnhardt didn't win, but he ended the day in defiance, forcing Labonte to spin awkwardly as he crossed the finish line.

Even when it appeared he had crashed out of events, he sometimes refused to quit. In his well-documented ambulance escape, Earnhardt finished the 1997 Daytona 500 after being taken to an ambulance after his car had flipped in the backstretch of the speedway.

Frustrated by the circumstances of the day, Earnhardt walked out of the ambulance, returned to his tattered car and drove it across the finish line.

Even in his final NASCAR win last October at Talladega, Earnhardt was victorious in grand fashion. The day after Tony Roper died from injuries suffered in a Truck series crash at Texas Motor Speedway, Earnhardt was in 18th place in the waning laps.

The race was the first in which NASCAR used a new set of

aerodynamic rules, established to reduce space. Despite his disdain for the new rules, Earnhardt got to the front and earned his 76th career title. The win gave him the sixth-most career titles in race history, the most for an active driver.

"Dale Earnhardt was the greatest driver who ever lived — he could do things with a car no one else could," said former NASCAR champion Ned Jarrett, the father of Dale Jarrett. "He leaves a big, big void here that will be very hard to fill."

To the very end

Even during the final two races of his life, Earnhardt demonstrated his unique racing style. In the IROC race and Daytona 500 preamble, Eddie Cheever and Earnhardt bumped, with Earnhardt falling out of contention. But when the race was over, Earnhardt drove up behind Cheever, spun him out of control and the two drivers exchanged words.

Cheever was apologetic after the race, commenting, "The last thing I need is a feud with Dale Earnhardt."

In his fatal Daytona 500 finale, Earnhardt bumped Sterling Marlin to go into the lead on the 40th lap. He and friend Jeff Gordon "traded paint" at one point during the race. And then there were several instances when The Intimidator nudged rookies Ron Hornaday and Kurt Busch. In Busch's instance, Earnhardt, frustrated by his inability to pass the young and slow driver, finally made his move. While he sped away, Earnhardt made an obscene gesture out of the window.

Earnhardt, who led the race four times for a total of 17 laps, made one pass by maneuvering his car down to the bottom of the concrete oval where he saw an apparent opening. As two wheels slipped into the infield grass, track radio announcer Eli Gould shouted, "The grass is just green asphalt to Earnhardt."

On the final stretch, many observers felt Earnhardt slowed down to fend off others from possibly defeating Michael Waltrip, whom he thought of as a younger brother, and his son, Dale Earnhardt, Jr.

Such was Earnhardt's legacy. When details of the crash that took his life began to unfold, fellow racers couldn't believe The Intimidator wouldn't race again. "After the race was over, I heard things didn't look very good, but, man, Earnhardt?" driver Jeremy Mayfield said. "You figure he'll bounce right back."

A few hours after Earnhardt's death, fans began arriving to mourn at Earnhardt race shops and family residences in North Carolina. Flags were hung at half-staff in several locations. Burning candles and flowers were positioned around photographs of the deceased driver as tributes.

And there were several handmade signs, one of which perhaps best addressed the loss of Dale Earnhardt.

"It's hard to lose a hero, but at least we've got the memories," the sign read. "RIP, Intimidator." ∎

Bumping and nudging opponents was business as usual for the No. 3 Chevy, which spent plenty of time in the repair garage.

Bittersweet
Memories

FOR EARNHARDT,
DAYTONA WAS A
PLACE OF TRIUMPH,
FRUSTRATION AND,
ULTIMATELY, TRAGEDY

By James Raia

During his legendary career, Dale Earnhardt competed on famed race tracks and on circuits he would have likely just as soon forgotten. But the Daytona International Speedway was his favorite and most successful venue. In a career that spanned five decades, Earnhardt won 32 races at the track — nearly half of his career victories — and more than any other NASCAR driver. Through bad luck and various other twists of fate, Daytona was both Earnhardt's hell and his most cherished place away from his North Carolina home.

Earnhardt peers out at the site of his
greatest triumphs and defeats:
Daytona International Speedway.

Bittersweet
Memories

Despite victories in other events at the speedway and four second-place finishes in the last eight years at the Daytona 500, it took Earnhardt 20 attempts until he captured the event he longed to win throughout his career. Earnhardt claimed the 1998 Daytona 500, his only victory of that season in 33 races. But it was a race that capsulized a career that emerged from boyhood memories of watching his father race to Earnhardt's emergence as an elder statesman of the NASCAR circuit.

Earnhardt sometimes was a man of few words, sometimes not. He was both after winning the Daytona 500. "Yes!, Yes!, Yes!,"

he exclaimed as he popped his head out of the No. 3 Chevrolet on Victory Lane. Earnhardt's victory was claimed at an average speed of 172.712 mph, the third-fastest in the race's history. It also occurred as if planned with perfect timing for NASCAR's 50th anniversary season. The win also allowed Earnhardt to earn a record $1,059,015 and end his nearly two-year winless streak of 59 races. "Everybody over the last week has said, 'This is your year,' " Earnhardt said in the next day's edition of *The Charlotte Observer.* "Man, they were so adamant about it. They knew something I didn't, I reckon."

Although he had already won 70 races in his career, the Daytona 500 title had eluded him for so long, his emotions could finally be displayed — sort of. "I cried a little bit in the race car on the way to the checkered flag," Earnhardt said. "Well, maybe not cried, but at least my eyes watered up."

A memorable day

Unlike many of his disappointing last-lap finishes at Daytona, Earnhardt's historic win was not anti-climactic, but it was void of any last-second heroics or the frustrations that often marked his career. Earnhardt took the lead on the 140th of the 200-lap race when he passed teammate Mike Skinner on Turn 4. He retained the lead when he pitted for fuel and right-side tires with less than 27 laps to go.

"We just kept playing our cards," Earnhardt recalled. "The others would go this way or that way and I would go with them. What I was hoping for was that they'd stay close in line and when it got down to five [laps] to go, they would start racing behind me. That made me feel better because I could pick who I wanted to dice with."

Racing under ever-darkening skies, a threat of rain and Earnhardt's long history of late-race mishaps, added to the drama. But the luck of the day finally went Earnhardt's way. "When we came out in front on that pit stop, I just knew that Dale Earnhardt was going to lead the race the rest of the way," said Richard Childress, the car owner.

With one lap left, the Ford driven by →

AP/WIDE WORLD PHOTO

The Intimidator became the celebrator after claiming the long-awaited Daytona 500 victory.

Bittersweet
Memories

AP/WIDE WORLD PHOTO

Jimmy Spencer collided into John Andretti's Pontiac. Andretti's car spun, knocking into Lake Speed's Ford. The crash brought out the third caution of the day. As a result, Earnhardt, who led the race five times for a total of 105 laps, won ironically under a caution flag.

A record crowd of 185,000 witnessed the highly emotional race on the famous high-banked trioval track. Even the crews and representatives of other teams stood in unison and cheered as Earnhardt ended his one racing stigma. Well-wishers in the pit row rushed out to congratulate the long overdue winner. There were smiles and laughter and tears of joy. Earnhardt then drove his car into the field and did two "doughnuts" before pulling into Victory Lane for a long celebration.

"It was my time," Earnhardt said. "I have been passed on the last lap, I have run out of gas and I have had a cut tire. I don't care how we won it, but that we won it.

"It's a feeling you can't replace," he continued. "It's eluded us for so many years. The drama and excitement of it all has built so much over the years. There have been a lot of emotions played out down here at Daytona with the letdowns we've had."

A relationship begins

Three years after he began his NASCAR career, Earnhardt first raced at Daytona on July 4, 1978. He finished seventh in the Pepsi 400 while driving a Ford. But while there were many victories and many other tracks, Earnhardt's affinity for Daytona's 2.5-mile super speedway and its 31-degree bank track rapidly grew as his career progressed.

Since 1989, Earnhardt had claimed at least one race every year at Daytona. And even in the final races of his career, three months shy of age 50, he wanted more wins. In the International Race of Champions (IROC) two days prior to the 2001 Daytona 500, Earnhardt was racing for the lead. But Eddie Cheever ran him into the grass on the first turn and catapulted Dale Jarrett to the win.

Although Earnhardt and Cheever exchanged words, The Intimidator remained unscathed. "I've got one shot left," Earnhardt said, in an eerie reference to the pending final race of his life. "Maybe it's a good omen for the 500."

As it turned out, the omen was anything but good. When Earnhardt crashed and was killed in the waning seconds of the 2001 Daytona 500, it marked the end of the most unique relationship between a driver and a race track in racing history. "NASCAR has lost its greatest driver, ever," said Bill France Jr., the circuit's chairman.

But the track in which he lost his life was also the track of his greatest success and ➜

Jubilant triumphs and bitter disappointments were par for the course at Daytona.

Bittersweet
Memories

frustrations. It was also the venue in which he earned a good percentage of his record career earnings of $41,640,462.

Earnhardt's legacy and his death brought out emotional comments from the racing world. But many of his associates had similarly admiring and respectful thoughts.

They were all perhaps summed succinctly by Dan Davis of Ford Racing. "Dale Earnhardt transcended NASCAR," Davis said.

It may have taken Earnhardt 20 attempts to win the race he coveted the most, but there were plenty of other crowns on the Daytona circuit. He won the Pepsi 400 twice and also captured seven Busch Grand Nationals titles, seven Goody's 300s, 12 Twin 125 events, including 10 straight from 1990-1999; six Budweiser Shootouts and six IROC titles. Earnhardt particularly enjoyed the IROC races, since it gave him the opportunity to showcase his driving talents to drivers from other racing circuits.

But for as many wins as he accumulated despite a career replete with injuries, there were nearly as many disappointments. The Daytona 500 win made up for the other disappointments, but it may have been Earnhardt's losses that helped build his legacy as much as his career of dominance.

In the 1986 Daytona 500, he ran out of tricks, allowing Geoff Bodine to win. In 1990, Earnhardt led for most the race. But he suffered a cut tire that sprung rookie Derrike Cope the crown.

The following year, Earnhardt could have been on his way to victory again when an accident with the late Davey Allison pushed Ernie Irvan to the win. In two more instances, Earnhardt finished second by a combined time of .73 seconds. In 1995, he was the runner-up to Sterling Marlin by .61 seconds.

The following year, his margin of loss was only .12 seconds to Dale Jarrett. "Racing someone and running second hasn't been too bad," said Earnhardt. "Letdowns of being dominant and not winning really worked on Richard and me. To come out here and race in a competitive race and not be that dominant, but still be dominant enough to lead most of the race and win, makes you feel proud of what you've accomplished with your team. We worked hard to win the Daytona 500."

That is what Dale Earnhardt always did. He worked hard, always with two things in mind: driving fast and winning. ■

Continu
a Lega

EARNHARDT JR. WILL STRIVE TO
UPHOLD HIS FAMILY'S TRADITION

By Jason Wilde

It was only a dream. It came to Dale Earnhardt Jr. last month, a few weeks before he was to race in his second Daytona 500, the same race that it took his legendary father, Dale Earnhardt Sr., 20 years to win.

"I'm pretty confident that I'm going to win the Daytona 500. Because I've dreamed about it so much," he said. "You can call me crazy, but I'll be talking to you at the post-race interview, talking about how I did it."

In the dream, he did it the easy way. "Out front all day," he said. "It was so real, it was crazy."

And where was his legendary father? "He wasn't there," Earnhardt Jr. said.

Sadly, tragically, when Earnhardt Jr. crossed the finish line in the 2001 Daytona 500 — second, 0.124 of a second behind teammate Michael Waltrip — his father was not there. Dale Sr.'s familiar black No. 3 Chevrolet had crashed seconds before the checkered

flag, less than half a mile from the finish line, into the concrete outside retaining wall in Turn 4 of Daytona International Speedway. He died instantly.

Suddenly, Earnhardt Jr. had lost the man who meant everything to him. Instead of celebrating Dale Earnhardt Inc.'s 1-2 finish, Dale Jr. crossed the finish line, parked his car at pit row and immediately tried to get to the scene of the crash he'd seen in his rearview mirror. And this was no dream.

Last season, Dale Jr. wrote a story about his father that he planned to post on NASCAR's official web site. Before he sent it in, though, he wanted to read it to his father. So one day after a meeting in his dad's office, he stayed behind. As soon as the doors were shut, he started reading the story, part of which reads, "This man [Dale Sr.] could lead the world's finest army. He has wisdom that knows no bounds. No fire could burn his character, no stone could break it. Every →

Continuing a Legacy

step he takes has purpose. Every walk has reason."

"That was something special," Earnhardt Sr. told *Sports Illustrated* last December. "You know, he tells me he loves me all the time, but when you hear something like that, well, it really gets you. Racing, and just being around each other more, has brought us closer."

And now, just like that, the father is gone. And the son must somehow find the strength to go on racing without him. It won't be easy.

A victory in the 500 would have helped Earnhardt Jr. forget the disappointment of the second half of his rookie season. Earnhardt Jr. joined his father in the Winston Cup Series last year, won two races plus the non-points Winston race — NASCAR's version of an all-star game — in the season's first half. But Earnhardt Jr. did not have a top-10 finish in the last 21 races. He wound up 16th in the points standings.

"There were a lot of things. We had a lot of problems. We all had ego problems, we all had personality problems," Earnhardt Jr. said of himself and his team. "We just all lost respect for each other, me and my teammates, and me and my crew. We just kind of let it go to our heads, the success we had at the first half of the year. And we couldn't repeat that like we wanted to. We never really pointed fingers at each other, but we did let each other know we weren't happy."

But this was the start of a new season, a new year. Everything was going to be different. And now, just one race into the season, he must go on with a heavy heart. He'd lost more than just a race. He'd lost the owner of his team, the man who raised him in the sport. He'd lost his father.

Dale Jr., 26, is the second child from his father's second marriage and the third of Dale Sr.'s four children. Dale Jr.'s sister, Kelly, is two years older. Dale Jr.'s older half-brother — Kerry, the oldest, from Dale's first marriage — also races occasionally on the Busch circuit. They also have a younger half-sister, Taylor, from Dale's third marriage to Teresa, who was at Dale Sr.'s bedside when he was pronounced dead.

"I never thought Dale Jr. was going to be a driver," Dale Sr. said. "He never seemed to have the interest. He wasn't one of those kids who always wanted to be around the garage, to see how things worked. What's happened has kind of surprised me."

"I always wanted to be a driver," Dale Jr. countered. "There always was this idea, though, that you had to sweep the floor for a year before you ever got a chance to touch a wrench. I didn't want to sweep the floor." ➜

Earnhardt Jr. finished in second place, only 0.124 of a second behind Waltrip at this year's Daytona 500.

Continuing a Legacy

Asked during his Winston Cup rookie year about working for his dad, Dale Jr. replied: "Just like every other boss. He ain't no super jerk or nothin'. Actually, having him for a father is pretty cool, because of what he knows, because of everything he's done and his experience."

But being close to his father had been a challenge throughout Dale Jr.'s life. Until he was 6, Dale Jr. and Kelly lived with their mother. When they moved into their father's house in 1980, Dale Sr. was winning his first Winston Cup championship, in his second year on the circuit. And as NASCAR grew in popularity and his father's schedule grew more hectic, time with Dad was in even shorter supply.

And when they did manage to get together, it was hard. "I always wanted Dale Jr. to get an education," Dale Sr. said. "I always talked about that. My biggest regret is that I dropped out of school in ninth grade. My father told me it was a mistake. I just wouldn't listen. I wanted to make sure Dale Jr. didn't make the same mistake. It was a battle, but we got him through."

"Education was such a big thing. So I graduated from high school, and where was my father? He didn't come to graduation. He was in a race somewhere," Dale Jr. said. "I understand now, of course, but I was looking forward to holding that diploma in his face. Except he wasn't there. He was at some other end of the earth."

Dale Sr. had also grown up in a racing family, but that was long before the sport had taken off. Back then,

A victory at Daytona would have eased the pain of a difficult second half of Dale Jr.'s rookie season.

when his father, Ralph Earnhardt, won the 1956 NASCAR Sportsman championship, the races were usually on Saturday nights in North Carolina and Georgia. After Ralph's races, the family would drive home together and have a party. There wasn't the father-son separation that there was when Dale Jr. was growing up.

But racing finally brought father and son together. As a kid, Dale Jr. would go to the go-kart track, where his father would stand a few feet from the wall, making him drive through a narrow space in between. With each lap, Dale Sr. would stand a little closer to the wall, to teach his son how to take the best angle on the turns. Dale Jr. became serious about racing in 1991, his senior year of high school, and Dad would bring Dale Jr. through the short-track ranks and into the Busch Series full-time in 1998, when he won the first of two championships.

"I'm going through a lot of the things my father's been through, and I'm starting to understand him more," Dale Jr. said earlier this year. "I feel we're able to relate to each other easier."

But that's not to say that being on the same track together week-in and week-out hasn't resulted in the two having their rough moments. Like last year during Dale Jr.'s first Daytona 500, when he ended up 13th and his father finished 21st.

The two raced with each other — or within a few positions of each other — during much of the second half of the race, pushing their way into the top five at times with the son racing behind his dad. But as the end neared, Earnhardt Jr. got antsy. He left his father behind, opting to work with other drivers while his father struggled. Earnhardt Jr. passed his father on lap 177 of the 200-lap race with the help of race-winner Dale Jarrett.

"When me and dad were hooked up in the draft, we really couldn't get anybody to stay behind us and couldn't get anybody to work with us," ➔

Continuing a Legacy

Earnhardt Jr. said afterward. "So that's when I thought, 'Get out of the way! Get out of the way!' I just wanted everybody to get out of the way. I was willing to hook up [and draft] with anybody."

"I thought he would be the first one to help me, but he was the last person who wanted to stay behind me. We did more racing than I wanted to. I wanted to stay with him and stay behind him. Then, everybody got to racing behind me and it was either pass or be passed."

Had father and son worked together, it could have been a family affair in Victory Lane. Earnhardt had moved to fourth and Little E to fifth, right on his father's bumper, and the two swapped

positions, sparring back and forth before the son struck out on his own. His father reacted angrily.

"He didn't work at all with anybody," Earnhardt said of his son. "He wanted to pass. That's all he wanted to do, so that's why he finished where he did."

Even less than a week before Dale Sr.'s death, father and son had an on-track run-in. In a group of cars battling for the lead with three laps remaining in the Budweiser Shootout, Earnhardt Jr. lost inside position to his father and Rusty Wallace. Earnhardt Jr. dropped from second to sixth, losing any chance at victory.

"I helped [my dad] out a few times, and he got me in the lead a few times.

But when it comes down to the last 10 laps, ain't nobody going to be helping you," Earnhardt Jr. said. Asked about his dad's late-race maneuver, Dale Jr. replied diplomatically, "I was surprised."

But there were some great father-and-son moments, too. For his second Winston Cup victory last May, Earnhardt Jr. passed his father with 31 laps to go in the Pontiac Excitement 400 and held on to become the first repeat winner of the season.

Last August, Dale Sr., Dale Jr. and Kerry all ran in the Pepsi 400, just the second race in NASCAR Winston Cup history where a father raced against two sons. Dad finished sixth, while Dale Jr., who started on the pole, finished 31st. Kerry, making his Cup debut, finished last after crashing on lap 6.

And last Father's Day weekend in Long Pond, Pa., Kerry won the Pocono ARCA 200 for the first victory of his career — with his dad on the radio, talking him through it — while Sr. and Jr. started side-by-side on the eighth row at the Pocono 500.

And earlier this month, Dale Sr. and Jr. teamed up with Andy Pilgrim and Kelly Collins for the Rolex 24 Hours of Daytona and finished fourth. Afterward, Dale Jr. admitted that there's a difference between being his dad's employee and his teammate.

"He expects a lot from me as a driver for his Winston Cup team, but he expects even more from me now because I'm his teammate," Dale Jr. said. "Now I know what Mike Skinner has been going through. Dad's such a competitor."

But it was in Dale Sr.'s final race that he did what some thought was out of character for the fiercely competitive, win-at-all-costs Intimidator. Running third on the final lap, Earnhardt decided not to go for the win. Instead, he chose to keep the rest of the field at bay and let his son and Waltrip fight it out for the

Now, Dale Jr. must somehow find the strength to go on racing without the man who taught him.

victory while he protected them from the contenders in pursuit.

Seconds later, he was dead. And while the son will face the challenges of replacing his legendary father in the years ahead, even if he manages to win seven Cup titles like his dad did, it won't be the same without him.

"The highlight of my life is seeing the smile on my daddy's face," Earnhardt Jr. once said. "I mean, that is what this is all about: Making people happy. It does my heart good to know how happy he is, how happy my team is." ■

Dale Sr. said that racing and being together brought him closer to his son.

Where
Legends
are
Made

Nothing else matches the tradition, spectacle

By Roland Lazenby

Among the sad facts to emerge from Dale Earnhardt's final lap is this: The legend of Daytona International Speedway only grows. Nothing can diminish it.

Not even tragedy.

"Daytona is Daytona. It's the first race; it's the biggest race," explains Eddie Wood, part owner of the Wood Brothers Racing team that's won 11 races at Daytona over the years. "It's the Super Bowl of racing."

Winning there brings the biggest rewards in racing, which means that winning there demands the biggest risks in all of racing. Always has. Always will.

Yet never again will a driver execute a draft move in the final lap of the Daytona 500 without bringing to mind both Earnhardt's demise and his fierce aggressiveness. Now they are a permanent part of a Daytona character that is rich and deep and troubling and majestic. Over the years, fans and competitors at the 2.5-mile track have seen it all, the great moments, the heart-spinning finishes, all mixed with the range of setbacks and losses that life on

# of Daytona

Above, David Pearson holds the Daytona trophy after his 1976 victory. At left, the engine on Curtis Turner's 1966 Chevy blows up during the 1967 race.

Where
Legends
are
Made

the NASCAR circuit brings — the untimely deaths of loved ones and close friends, the smashed cars and fractured plans, the off-track battles for drivers and sponsors.

Few have seen more than Glen Wood, the patriarch of the Wood Brothers clan. Wood's personal history spans the explosive growth of stock-car racing, beginning on the dirt tracks of the South just after World War II and running through the modern boom of big-time NASCAR competition.

Of the Woods' many victories, some the greatest have come at Daytona. They first won on the big track in 1963 in a freakish turn of events. In the days leading up to the race, the Woods' hopes seemed dashed when their qualifying driver, Marvin Panch, was badly injured in a preliminary race.

Panch was pulled from a fiery crash by another lesser-known driver, Tiny Lund. Deeply grateful, Panch asked the Woods to reward Lund's lifesaving efforts by letting him drive their Ford in the Daytona showcase. The Woods

The Daytona 500 is the Super Bowl of racing

agreed, and Lund responded by pulling off a major upset and winning the race.

That 1963 Daytona finish is considered the event that established Ford as a top competitor in stock-car racing.

Asked for his favorite Daytona memory, the elder Wood cites his team's 1976 victory, often described as the most exciting finish in the track's illustrious history. I've never quite had a feeling of excitement like I did that day," Glen Wood said.

The Wood Brothers' Mercury, driven by David Pearson, had battled Richard Petty through most of the race. From the pits, Eddie Wood kept contact with Pearson on the radio. "Richard and David had been going at each other all day long," Eddie recalled. "It was just those two. On the radio, Pearson told me, 'We'll go down to the last lap and have it out.' And that's how it happened.

"As they came off of Turn 2 in the last lap, David said, 'I don't know if I can get him or not.' Then, as he got to Turn 3, he told me, 'I got him.'"

But at Turn 4, Petty attempted to push past Pearson and bumped him cutting back in. Both cars spun out just yards short of the finish line. Petty's car died, but somehow Pearson kept the Mercury Cyclone alive. Frantically, the Petty crew tried to push his car across the line. ➜

Richard Petty was a winner in 1971 (top right), but not so lucky in '75.

Where Legends are Made

The collision, meanwhile, had left Pearson a bit disoriented; he couldn't see Petty's car. "Has he crossed the line?" Pearson yelled over the radio. "No," Eddie Wood yelled back through the radio.

"Well, I'm coming," Pearson said and gunned the Cyclone over the line to the Woods' biggest win.

Like the Woods, most competitors in racing count their victories at Daytona as their most cherished. And often most controversial, because of the daring required.

Take for example Jeff Gordon's big move in 1999 to edge Earnhardt and win the 500 for the second time in three years.

"With the camera angle that they had on that, it really looked a lot closer than it actually was," Gordon recalled. Rusty Wallace had the lead late until Gordon made a daring pass, which left Wallace fussing.

Daytona's character is rich, deep, troubling and majestic

"We all made a bunch out of it at that particular time," Wallace recalled. "The fans did, I did and whatever. You look back at it right now and it's no big deal."

Bobby Hamilton crashed in the backstretch of Lap 175 of the 200-lap race which brought out a caution and set up the turn of events. Wallace and teammate Jeremy Mayfield, whose Fords had been running first and second when Hamilton crashed, chose not to pit for fuel and tires, but Gordon and the other contenders did. Then they lined up behind Wallace and Mayfield for the 22 laps remaining.

Mayfield soon lost ground, but Wallace held on until he pulled the lead draft toward Turn 1 on Lap 190.

That's when Gordon headed his Chevy for the low side of the track to make a move for the lead. He crossed the yellow line marks at pit road's exit, almost hit Ricky Rudd's Ford as it was coming back onto the track, and still managed to pass Wallace. Once he got the lead, Gordon never gave it up.

"It certainly was an exciting move, but when you're going for a Daytona 500 win, you've got to make moves like that sometimes," Gordon said. "It's just kind of the way drafting works at Daytona and when you get momentum, you've got to take advantage of that momentum.

"If you're talking about coming down with a few laps to ➜

Pete Hamilton and Sharon Brown celebrate Hamilton's Daytona win in 1970.

go, then you're going to take some risks. I certainly wouldn't make a move like that 10 laps into the race, but I'm certainly going to do it again if I had to near the end."

"I think it was definitely a daring move," Mayfield said. "But I don't think Gordon would have done anything to jeopardize anybody. I mean if he knew that he couldn't make it or it was really going to be a really high risk, he wouldn't have done it."

"It's a move that's worked for me several times and it's probably the only place on the race track where you can do something like that," Gordon said of the low side of Turn 1. "Of course I wasn't expecting Ricky Rudd to be there, either. It would have been a perfect plan had he not been there, but because he was it made things a little hairy. Luckily, he got out of the way and I made it through there all right."

Winning at Daytona brings the biggest risks in racing

The low side of Turn 1 was also where Gordon dove to pass Bill Elliott for the lead late in the 1997 Daytona 500. Gordon took the low path while Hendrick Motorsports teammates Terry Labonte and Ricky Craven went outside around Elliott's Ford. Mayfield wound up 20th after his flat tire but was still close enough to the front to have a good view of Gordon's pass of Wallace.

Dale Jarrett has three career wins in NASCAR'S biggest race, the last coming in 2000 when he passed Johnny Benson with four laps to go.

"When I got involved in Winston Cup racing I had the dream that everybody else does of one day being in that Victory Lane and having a Daytona 500 trophy," Jarrett told the media afterward.

Only Richard Petty and Cale Yarborough, with four Daytona 500 victories, have now won the event more than Jarrett and Bobby Allison, who also won the race three times.

Jarrett's 2000 victory celebration also was marked by an on-track confrontation from Martin, upset by Jarrett's manuevers on Lap 187 as they fought to move past Benson's Pontiac.

"Mark had radioed and asked if he went high would I go with him, and I said yes," Jarrett explained. "We tried it the lap before and didn't get a very good run. Nothing else ➔

Where
Legends
are
Made

was said then. We came down through the trioval the next time, went into Turn 1, Mark went high and I went into the corner high with every intention of going with Mark."

But Jarrett saw Burton going low and went for the opportunity.

"I've got to protect my position at that point," Jarrett said. "I didn't lie to Mark Martin. I know he felt like that and there's nothing I can say that's going to change his mind. But when I looked up and saw the 99 (Burton) knowing he had the 94 (Elliott) right behind him, I was getting ready to lose my spot for sure."

After getting past Martin, Jarrett still had Benson to deal with. "I knew that he was going to try to block me," Jarrett said. "I faked high and he went up there, and as soon as I saw him move up the race track I cut my car dead left. I was committed. If I would have had to go to the apron, which I almost had to, that's where I was going."

The Daytona 500 is a complex mix of victory, heart-spinning finishes, setbacks and tragedy

---

Although his success at the 500 was limited to his one victory, Earnhardt himself loved the Daytona speedway, loved the demands it placed on his talent and that of other drivers.

He last won there in the International Race of Champions series in 2000. "I'm 48 and moving," Earnhardt said at the time. "I have a lot of racing yet before I quit or slow down. To win a race of cars built as equally as they can be built and with drivers that are champions. You race against a lot of wins and a lot of championships, and it makes you feel good to be competitive in that kind of racing and even win it.

"Winning it here at Daytona makes it even more so for me because this is a race track I love to race at."

Now that Earnhardt fire is inextricably linked with Daytona. And the legacy deepens. ∎

Driver's last prayer was for safety, wisdom preacher says

By ALLEN G. BREED
Associated Press

RALEIGH, N.C. — Most race day Sundays for the past 13 years, the Rev. Max Helton has stood at the side of Dale Earnhardt's black No. 3 Chevy and led a prayer.

Sunday's Daytona 500 was no exception — Earnhardt insisted on it.

Helton said he gathered on the track with Earnhardt's wife, Teresa, and Richard Childress, the car's owner.

"We held hands through his window," said Helton, a Presbyterian minister and founder of Motor Racing Outreach.

"He says, 'Just pray that I'll be wise in putting the car at the right place at the right time ... and be able to drive with wisdom.' And we did pray about that. And we did pray for safety."

Racing fans feel a giant void

Towns built around racing show their respect for one of NASCAR's greatest drivers.

By JENNA FRYER
The Associated Press

MOORESVILLE, N.C. — A single black balloon broke free from the wrought iron fence surrounding the sprawling complex housing Dale Earnhardt's racing teams.

A security guard caught the balloon and retied it next to the growing memorial of personalized tributes left by fans Monday in memory of the seven-time Winston Cup champion who died the day before in a crash at the Daytona 500.

A sign said the compound was "respectfully closed today." Still, employees of Dale Earnhardt Inc. solemnly filed in, past the security officers posted at every gate.

"It ain't too good in there. Everyone's trying their best," said Cam Ramey, the security chief.

Dale Earnhardt Jr., who finished second in Sunday's race, emerged from the complex shortly before noon in a black pickup truck. He was driven across the street and up a private drive to his home.

"He's holding up as best he can under the circumstances," said Steve Crisp, who drove Earnhardt Jr. to his house.

"There is a lot of character in that family and in that organization," said H.A. "Humpy" Wheeler, president of Lowe's Motor Speedway in nearby Concord.

He said he thought the teams still would participate in this weekend's Dura-Lube 400 at North Carolina Speedway in Rockingham.

Hundreds of fans left poems, letters and pictures at the compound, quietly taking in the scene, occasionally wiping away a tear. "Forever A Champion," one sign said.

When a team wins a race, tradition at Dale Earnhardt Inc. calls for a checkered flag to fly in front of the complex until the next race begins the following week. On Monday, the flag was at half-staff, representing both Michael Waltrip's victory at Daytona and Earnhardt's death on the last lap of the race.

"It's like Superman is dead," said Craig Freshwater, who made the 30-mile trip from Charlotte to pay his respects. "Heroes aren't supposed to die."

"He was a guy you either loved or loved to hate," said Earnhardt fan Gary Farabee. "But it's just not the same this morning. It just doesn't feel right.

"Over the last year, I think he exposed his inner self, his softer side, a little more," Farabee said. "I don't think I pulled for him as much as a racer as I pulled for him as a man."

When Earnhardt finished, he squeezed Helton's hand, as he always did. But this time, something was different.

"I noticed it at that particular time, that he seemed to squeeze my hand a little longer than he normally does," Helton said in a telephone interview Wednesday.

After the race, Helton was in a prayer circle with the same people. Only this time it was at a hospital, and his old friend was dead.

"No one expected, I think, Dale Earnhardt to die in a race car," he said. "Maybe in a plane crash, maybe in some other way; but not in a race car. Because he was so good and he's been through so many crashes and walked away from them that seemed a lot worse than the one he was in and which took his life."

Helton, whose ministry has traveled the NASCAR circuit since 1988, said he didn't think much about Earnhardt's gesture at the time, because The Intimidator was always surprising him. He remembers one instance when he greeted Earnhardt in the victory circle.

"Man, he grabbed me by the neck and pulled my head in and said, 'Let's pray and thank God for this victory,'" Helton recalled. "He was just that way."

Helton was waiting in the victory circle Sunday and watching the race on a Jumbotron when the accident occurred. But he didn't think it

looked "that horribly bad" and went to congratulate winner Michael Waltrip.

Helton was walking casually through the garage when someone told him it was serious. He was ushered into a waiting police car and rushed to nearby Halifax Medical Center.

"They were still working on him at the time, and I was there with them when the doctors told them, 'Listen, we've done everything we can do,'" Helton said. "I was right there by his side at the table in the trauma room."

Helton led Teresa Earnhardt, Dale Jr. and Childress in a prayer beside the trauma table.

"We were praying that God would give sustaining grace and that God would give his strength and wisdom," he said. "We were really hurting, and we talked about in our prayer, even confessed the fact that, yes, we're really hurt and we're deeply saddened by this, and we're asking for God's saving grace through this."

Helton said some might think it odd that Earnhardt's final prayer for safety would be answered with a fatal wreck. But he doesn't see it that way.

"If you look at that, I mean, God really watched over him and cared for him, because he took him on," he said. "You know, that's the ultimate safety. He'll never hurt again."

Festive Daytona scene turns sour

AP/Wide World Photos

DAYTONA BEACH, Fla. — Inside the museum next to the track where Dale Earnhardt died, roses started piling up on top of a black Monte Carlo pace car that looks hauntingly like The Intimidator's.

In restaurants across the street, patrons left suddenly when they heard the news.

The city of Daytona Beach, normally home to a rowdy, drunken Mardi Gras scene after the Daytona 500, fell into mourning Sunday night after hearing one of auto racing's greats had been killed in a crash on the final lap.

"I can't stop crying," said Patty Miesel, a race fan from Pittsburgh. "I've been crying ever since I heard the news. We love all of the NASCAR drivers, but Earnhardt had a special place in our heart."

She and her husband went to a souvenir shop after they heard the news and had a special T-shirt made. It has a big No. 3 on it and the words, "Winners come and go, but legends live forever."

Colleagues of The Intimidator — as Earnhardt was known far and wide — were equally shocked.

"No matter where it happens or how it happens or even how prepared you think you might be for it, losing somebody close to you hurts," said Kyle Petty, whose son Adam died last year in a wreck. "My heart just breaks for the family."

Petty's teammate, John Andretti, added: "I feel like somebody kicked me in the chest. I'm stunned. And I'm really sad. That's about all I can say."

Race fan Ken Satherfield of South Carolina fought the traffic and made his way 30 miles up Interstate 95. When he heard the news, he turned back to join a troupe of fans for a vigil near Daytona International Speedway.

"We were really affected by this," Satherfield said. "We were very big Earnhardt fans."

Flags at the track and throughout the city were lowered to half-staff, as disbelief faded into teary-eyed acceptance.

"You never think anyone will get killed, but he was the last one you'd think that would happen to," said former NASCAR champion Ned Jarrett, wiping away tears.

He wasn't the only one who had trouble believing it had happened.

"After the race was over, I heard things didn't look very good," driver Jeremy Mayfield said. "But, man, Earnhardt? You figure he'll bounce right back. Your first thought is, 'Hey, he'll probably come back next week at Rockingham and beat us all.'"

Race fans Philip and Nancy Geraci of Massachusetts also turned back toward the speedway when they heard the news. Making their way back to the track to reminisce, they saw Earnhardt's trailer move down International Speedway Boulevard, with a police escort.

"It seemed like a funeral procession," Nancy Geraci said.

Reid Pelletier of Danbury, Conn., had just finished dinner when the news spread across the restaurant. People started crying. Some simply stopped eating and walked out.

Pelletier left and started driving toward the track. He was in his car and didn't plan to get out for a while.

"I'm emotionally shaken and in shock," he said. "I don't want to go to sleep now."

Earnhardt's legacy
will remain

By Mike Morris
Associated Press

"Dale, with us always."

That sign outside Daytona International Speedway speaks of the continuing love affair stock car racing has with Dale Earnhardt.

He was killed Sunday, one fateful corner away from another great afternoon at his favorite racetrack, dying from head injuries in a wreck on the last turn of the last lap of the Daytona 500.

The Intimidator won 34 times on Daytona's 2-mile oval, although it wasn't always easy.

For the first 19 years that he came to the sprawling track built by NASCAR founder Bill France Sr., he won nearly everything — the July Winston Cup race, qualifying races, Busch and IROC races.

Everything but the Daytona 500 — losing once when he blew a tire after dominating the race for 499 miles.

That finally changed in 1998, when Earnhardt gleefully took the checkered flag in NASCAR's Super Bowl — punching his left fist out the window of his famed black No. 3 Chevrolet in triumph and spinning through the grass in a personal victory celebration.

As he drove slowly down pit lane toward Victory Circle, his smile gleaming beneath his bushy mustache, rival crews lined his path, slapping his palm and giving him thumbs up for what might have been the most awaited victory in NASCAR history.

Afterward, he showed a soft side that few knew he possessed.

"This one meant the world to me," Earnhardt said, his eyes shining. "People may think I'm tough and I don't care — and I am tough — but I'm human, too. I want to win every time I go out there, but there's some races that mean more than others. This is one of them."

Fans were rarely ambivalent about Earnhardt. Millions loved the dashing, cowboylike figure. Millions more vilified "The Man in Black."

Even more than his record-tying seven Winston Cup championships and his 76 victories — sixth all-time and the most among current drivers — Earnhardt's legacy is the role he played in NASCAR's rise to the mainstream of American culture.

His father, Ralph, was a rough and tumble stock car pioneer, never afraid of a fight — on or off the track.

The elder Earnhardt died of a heart attack while working on a race car in the garage of his North Carolina home. The 1956 NASCAR Sportsman division champion was 45.

Dale, 22 at the time, desperately wanted to follow his father into racing but had few resources. With only a ninth-grade education, he was working in a textile factory and twice divorced with three children by the age of 25.

What he had in abundance was an aggressive confidence that eventually translated to rides and racing victories.

Once he reached the top level of NASCAR for good, Earnhardt was an instant success, winning the Rookie of the Year title in 1979 and the first of his championships in 1980.

His racing prowess earned him millions of dollars on the track and many millions more from souvenir and memorabilia sales that dwarf those of his racing rivals.

"Image is everything," said Don Hawk, Earnhardt's former business manager. "People perceived Dale Earnhardt in different ways, good and bad. But they are always aware of him and care what he does, and they want a piece of him."

The success brought Earnhardt a lush, if hectic, lifestyle.

He flew to races, personal appearances and hunting and fishing trips in a private jet, occasionally relaxed aboard a 100-foot yacht, aptly christened "Sunday Money," and loved working around his 400-acre North Carolina farm, keeping an eye on the black Angus cattle, commercial chicken houses and quarterhorses when he had the chance.

He married Teresa Hunter in 1982, and added daughter Taylor to a family that already included daughter Kelly and sons Kerry and Dale Jr. from his previous marriages.

"He wasn't around a whole lot when I was growing up because he was off racing most of the time," Dale Jr. said. "But I always knew he cared about me and the other kids. He let us know in his way."

He owned a Chevrolet dealership and, although he continued to drive for longtime friend Richard Childress, Earnhardt decided to start his

own team, Dale Earnhardt Inc.

After starting with a Busch series program and a few Winston Cup races in 1997, the team moved Steve Park into NASCAR's top series in 1998, brought Dale Jr. in as his teammate in 2000 and added Michael Waltrip, the Daytona winner, as a third driver this season.

Earnhardt also was helping Kerry get his racing career into gear. But the arrival as a star of Dale Jr. — who won two straight Busch championships then two Winston Cup races as a rookie — particularly delighted him.

Dale Jr.'s success coincided with his father's resurgence as a title contender after a dry spell that had some wondering if his racing skills had declined.

At an age when most drivers talk about their accomplishments, the 49-year-old Earnhardt was confident he could win a record eighth title.

"Racing has been pretty much my whole life," Earnhardt said in a recent interview. "We're building something here, and my boys are here.

"I'm going to be racing for a while yet, but when the time comes, this is going to be what I do, run this team and stay involved in the sport."

It's true he's gone now. But his legacy won't leave any time soon.

Dale Earnhardt's LEGACY

AP/Wide World Photos

1951: Born in Kannapolis.

1973: Earnhardt's father, Ralph, dies at age 45 of a heart attack while working on a race car.

1975: Earnhardt makes his Winston Cup debut in the World 600 at Charlotte Motor Speedway. He started 33rd and finished 22nd in a Dodge owned by Ed Negre. He earned $2,245 and finished one spot ahead of his future boss, Richard Childress.

1979: He wins the Winston Cup Rookie of the Year title while driving for Rod Osterlund, the season that includes his first victory at Bristol.

1980: Earnhardt wins five races en route to his first Winston Cup championship. He's the only driver to win a series championship after being Rookie of the Year.

1981: Earnhardt struggles, failing to win a race or a pole. Osterlund sells the team in mid-season and Earnhardt quits. He drives for Childress the rest of the season.

1982: He joins Bud Moore's team. He wins at Darlington in April but fractures a knee in a crash at Talladega. He doesn't miss a race.

1983: He wins two races before bolting back to a car owned by Childress, with whom he'd spend the rest of racing career.

1984: He wins two races including one at Atlanta where newcomer Terry Schoonover is killed. "I'm sorry it happened, real sorry," Earnhardt said. "It's something you don't want to think about happening, and I try not to."

AP/Wide World Photos

1985: Earnhardt wins four races and finishes eighth in the season points race.

1986: He wins his second Winston Cup title with five victories.

1987: Earnhardt wins a third series title with 11 victories.

1989: He finishes second in the series, losing to Rusty Wallace by 12 points.

1990: Earnhardt earns a then-record $3 million in prize money while taking home a fourth Winston Cup title, 26 points ahead of Mark Martin.

1991: He takes a fifth series title.

1992: He finishes 12th in the season's points race, tying his worst showing of his Winston Cup career.

1993: Earnhardt wins a sixth Winston Cup championship.

1994: He ties Richard Petty's mark of seven Winston Cup titles.

1997: Earnhardt goes winless for the first time since 1981.

1998: He claims his only Daytona 500 victory, in his 20th attempt.

2000: He finishes second in the points race to Bobby Labonte. He wins his last race in October at Talladega, Ala., giving him 76 career victories.

2001: Earnhardt is killed in a crash during the last lap of the Daytona 500, while a car he owns, driven by Michael Waltrip, wins the race.

The sport **speaks out** on its lost legend

THE ASSOCIATED PRESS
Reaction to Dale Earnhardt's death Sunday in a crash on the last turn of the last lap of the Daytona 500:

* * *

"My heart is hurting right now. I would rather be any place right this moment than here. It's so painful." —race winner Michael Waltrip at his press conference. Waltrip drove a car owned by Earnhardt.

* * *

"This is understandably the hardest announcement I've ever had to make. We've lost Dale Earnhardt." —NASCAR president Mike Helton.

* * *

"NASCAR has lost its greatest driver ever, and I personally have lost a great friend." —NASCAR chairman Bill France Jr.

* * *

"It's always tragic, but this is our main guy. Today when they introduced him, he got the biggest applause there. He's the man, he is NASCAR Winston Cup racing. We haven't had something like this happen. We've got a lot of work to do at the track in the next three weeks (for the March 11 Cracker Barrel 400), but I don't feel like doing anything. I'm just numb. I've lost a great friend." —Ed Clark, president of Atlanta Motor Speedway.

* * *

"Dale Earnhardt was the greatest race car driver that ever lived. He could do things with a race car that no one else could. You never think anyone will get killed, but he was the last one you'd think that would happen to.

"He had a tremendous impact on NASCAR racing. He's done so much to help the sport get where it is today. He took the sport to new places. It's going to hard for anyone else to take it there. He leaves a big, big void here that will be very hard to fill." —Ned Jarrett, broadcaster, former driver and father of driver Dale Jarrett.

* * *

"No matter where it happens or how it happens or even how prepared you think you might be for it, losing somebody close to you hurts. My heart just breaks for Teresa and the family." —driver Kyle Petty. Petty's son, Adam, was killed last year in a crash during a Busch series practice session in New Hampshire.

* * *

"I don't know what to say. This is incredible, just incredible. I think everybody is just in shock right now. I didn't see much of what happened. After the race was over, I heard things didn't look very good but, man, Earnhardt. You figure he'll bounce right back. Your first thought is, hey, he'll probably come back next week at Rockingham and beat us all." —driver Jeremy Mayfield.

* * *

"It's just the way this sport is. That's the chances you take. It's unfortunate it happened to him. It just don't seem right. It's hard to believe. You don't think things like that will happen to drivers of his caliber.

"We're going to have to take a look at some of the safety issues. My driver tested the HANS (Head And Neck Safety) device over the summer and he will not get in the car without it now. If Dale had that on, we'd probably be looking at a different situation." —Todd Parrott, Dale Jarrett's crew chief.

* * *

"I feel like somebody kicked me in the chest. I'm stunned. And I'm really sad. That's about all I can say." —driver John Andretti.

* * *

"Like so many people around the world, I became a NASCAR fan because I became a Dale Earnhardt fan. Dale was someone I was proud to have my son look up to. We all have our memories we will cherish, memories of excitement, competitiveness and most of all memories of a great man. On behalf of the people of Alabama, I extend my thoughts and prayers to his family and friends." —Alabama Gov. Don Siegelman.

* * *

"Like many others, we were fans of Dale Earnhardt — certainly the driver, but especially the man. In spite of our intense rivalry, Dale Earnhardt has been a great friend to us and to all who have helped to make this sport great. Dale Earnhardt transcended NASCAR. His loss will have an effect on racing and its fans worldwide." —Dan Davis, director of Ford Racing Technology.

Always a Champion

Dale Earnhardt

1951 – 2001

The Final Farewe

Nation mourns the NASCAR legend

By David Fantle and Thomas Johnson

Perhaps not since the death of Elvis Presley in 1977 has a nation collectively mourned the loss of a celebrity.

Before his untimely and tragic death on the final lap of the Daytona 500 on February 18, 2001, Dale Earnhardt had long established himself as a racing legend. It's just so hard to let a legend go. Yes, he left doing what he lived to do, but the suddenness of the loss has left a void and deep sorrow in the racing world. In fact, the racing world has yet to come to grips with the death of the 49-year-old "Intimidator" or "Ironhead," another nickname taken from his father's own monicker, "Ironheart."

DALE EARNHARDT • DALE EA

Earnhardt Jr. prays with Motor Racing Outreach chaplain Max Helton before the start of the Dura Lube 400 in Rockingham, North Carolina.

NHARDT • DALE EARNHARDT

The Final Farewell

Fellow drivers and crew members dressed in black, friends and representatives from corporate sponsors gathered with Earnhardt's family to say goodbye.

A Presidential tribute

From main street U.S.A. to the White House, the nation is still grieving. President George W. Bush expressed his sadness at the death of Earnhardt and sent longtime friend and aide Joe Allbaugh to attend the first of several memorial services held Thursday, February 22.

"I am saddened by the untimely loss of this American legend and want to express my deepest sympathy to his family, friends and fans," Bush said in a statement. "Dale was an American icon who made great contributions to his sport," the president added. "Dale's legacy will live on for millions of Americans. He was an inspiration to many."

Bush, a racing fan and Earnhardt friend, sent his condolences to Earnhardt's widow, Teresa, on the day the seven-time Winston Cup champion was killed in the Daytona 500.

Flowers and tears

On Thursday, February 23, an invitation-only crowd of friends, family and racing cronies came to celebrate the life of fallen hero Earnhardt. Instead of tough-guy stories about The Intimidator, they heard heartfelt stories about the man.

Dale Beaver, a chaplain with the Motor Racing Outreach ministry, eulogized Earnhardt during the service. Beaver had done this before for others, but this must have been unusually difficult.

Fellow drivers and crew members dressed in black, friends and representatives from corporate sponsors gathered with Earnhardt's family to say goodbye. Beaver talked about a different side of the stock-car racing icon.

Beaver described his anxiety when he first met Earnhardt, interrupting his lunch to get permission for the driver's youngest daughter, Taylor, to go on a camping trip.

"I thought, 'He's eating bear and I'm going to be dessert,' " Beaver said.

But, he recalled, "I didn't come into the presence of a racing icon or an intimidating figure. I came into the presence of a dad, a father who was concerned about his daughter."

It drew the only laughter and smiles of an otherwise sullen service marked by sad, almost shell-shocked faces, but few tears a day after Earnhardt was buried in his hometown of Kannapolis, about 25 miles from Charlotte, North Carolina.

Earnhardt, a no-nonsense guy in life, would have probably wanted it this way. "A simple, solemn, brief memorial. And when it was over, everybody got ready for the next race at Rockingham," reported the Associated Press.

"If Dale was still here, he'd be going to Rockingham to race as hard as he knew how," driver and friend Rusty Wallace said. "That's what racers do."

An occasion reserved for few, the nationally televised memorial service ➔

AP/WIDE WORLD PHOTO

A memorial grows outside of the North Carolina Speedway.

DALE EARNHARDT • DALE E.

At the end of the service, Earnhardt's widow and wife of 18 years, Teresa, silent throughout the ceremony, walked to the front of the church, turned toward the crowd and blew two kisses.

drew an audience that watched the 22-minute service at Calvary Church which paid tribute to the racing great.

But unlike "traditional" funeral services, there was almost nothing displaying pictures, memorabilia or references to his legendary career save for a red, white and black floral arrangement in the shape of Earnhard'ts familiar No. 3 near the pulpit.

Perhaps the greatest connection was the sight of his children, including son, Dale Jr., who entered the church with Michael Waltrip, who won Daytona while driving one of Earnhardt's cars. "Little E," as his youngest son is known, has been mostly silent since his father's death with the exception of a brief news conference.

The only speakers to address the

2,500 invited guests were two ministers. Longtime friend Randy Owen, a member of the country band Alabama, sang and played his acoustic guitar.

At the end of the service, Earnhardt's widow and wife of 18 years, Teresa, silent throughout the ceremony, walked to the front of the church, turned toward the crowd and blew two kisses.

"Thank you, thank you," she whispered before she and 12-year-old Taylor were escorted out.

Racer Wallace said he attended the service to properly say goodbye to his friend and competitor. Like the rest of the NASCAR community, Wallace left for the Rockingham track after the service to prepare for yet another race, the Dura Lube 400.

"None of us were ready to let Dale go, and we will miss him terribly," Wallace said. "God only created one Dale Earnhardt and no one will ever replace him, neither in our sport or in our hearts."

Teresa Earnhardt expressed her gratitude to fans in an open letter published Friday, February 23, in *USA Today*.

"It would be easy at this time to get lost in the sadness of losing a

TAMI CHAPPELL/REUTERS

Teresa Earnhardt is escorted from Calvary Church by a North Carolina Highway Patrolman.

DALE EARNHARDT • DALE E.

Greg Rials of Savannah, Georgia, stands alone outside Calvary Church in Charlotte, North Carolina, while Earnhardt's memorial service is conducted inside.

loving husband, father and grandfather," she wrote. "However, I and our family, as well as everyone at Dale Earnhardt Inc., have chosen to take this time to reflect not on the sadness we feel today, but on the joy Dale Earnhardt the man brought to us and Dale Earnhardt the driver brought to so many fans for so many years.

"It is a joy that will carry us through the sadness and grief of this day and many days to come. For his fans, there simply was no one more sensational and with that I agree."

In her letter, she called herself "blessed" to have known both the public and private Earnhardt. "The public Dale Earnhardt wanted to be the best," she said. "The competitive drive that burned inside of him gave him the passion to win. If he was racing, he wanted to win the most races and championships. If he was fishing, he

wanted to catch the most fish.

"The private Dale Earnhardt, the husband and father and son and brother, wanted to be the best as well. He struggled with that at times. Emotions didn't come as easy to this man who stirred so much emotion in other people.

"But as his children grew and began making decisions of their own, he saw that most of the time, they made the decision by asking themselves, 'What would Dad do?' "

She thinks she knows what her husband would want to be remembered for.

"Remember the things about him that made you happy that you were his fan," she said. "Remember the man who loved life. He was the happiest person I know, and that can comfort us all."

Also attending the February 23 service were drivers Terry and Bobby

Labonte, Junior Johnson (who raced against Earnhardt's father Ralph), Jerry Nadeau, Bobby and Donnie Allison, and Sterling Marlin, who was involved in the fatal crash and received hate mail and telephone death threats from people who blamed him for Earnhardt's death. Earnhardt's No. 3 black Chevy made contact with Marlin's seconds before Earnhardt slammed into the wall.

"NASCAR will know that Earnhardt ain't in that race in Rockingham and it will hurt for a little while," Junior Johnson said. "It'll get by, but it's going to hurt. It's a sad day for NASCAR and the sport."

Bill France Jr., chairman of the board of the stock-car sanctioning body and son of NASCAR's founder, said after the service that the attention paid to Earnhardt's death "shows what kind of heroes NASCAR drivers have become." ➔

NHARDT • DALE EARNHARDT

"Dale Earnhardt was an icon, a legend," Daytona Beach Mayor Bud Asher said after the service. "His greatest successes were at Daytona Beach. He was a hero to the people here."

"As a rule, I don't get that close to the drivers just because of things like this," France said. "But some of them just jump out and grab you. Dale was one of those."

About 100 Earnhardt fans braved the rain and gathered outside the church, many of them wearing Earnhardt jackets and hats bearing his signature or No. 3.

One of the onlookers, truck driver Scott Poole, and three friends made a 7 1/2-hour trip from Hagerstown, Maryland. "This is a once-in-a-lifetime thing, just to be part of the memory," he said.

At the scene

In another memorial service, this one held in Daytona Beach, Florida, the site of Earnhardt's fatal crash, about 200 fans paid their last respects to their fallen hero at Central Baptist Church.

The AP reported that "Nursery school teacher Michelle Lindley delicately placed a paper heart adorned with a "3" on an altar.

"Thomas Hagerty brought a petition asking the city to name a bridge after Dale Earnhardt. Dozens signed it.

"Barbie Squires cried and patted the back of her 12-year-old son, Jesse Shriver, who held a box containing

action figures of Earnhardt and son Dale Earnhardt Jr."

Many of the attendees also were at Daytona International Speedway and witnessed the horrific accident that sent Earnhardt's car slamming into a concrete wall on the last turn of the last lap of the season-opening race.

"It's still very upsetting. I still don't believe it happened," Judy Tolland, a hairdresser from Temple, Pennsylvania who witnessed the crash, said. "It's not like him to get into a wreck and not come out of it."

Earnhardt, after 20 attempts, finally won the Daytona 500 in 1998.

"Dale Earnhardt was an icon, a legend," Daytona Beach Mayor Bud Asher said after the service. "His greatest successes were at Daytona Beach. He was a hero to the people here."

Asher proposed a lasting memorial to the racer by asking the city council that a pedestrian walkway to the Daytona International Speedway be named after Earnhardt.

Fans attending the ceremony laid out roses, notes and a No. 3 on the church altar behind framed photos of Earnhardt beside his car, with his son and holding a trophy. They wore T-shirts with Earnhardt's face on them

and lapel pins and windbreakers also with the No. 3.

"Dale has run, and run well, and now he's safe in the arms of God," the Rev. Hal Marchman, pastor emeritus at Central Baptist Church told the assembled.

Fans at the church also watched a video clip of Earnhardt's triumphant 1998 Daytona 500 race when members from every crew lined up to congratulate Earnhardt as he drove his car to the winner's circle.

"He has been such a big part of my life," said Tom Mulder, a 39-year-old limousine painter and Earnhardt fan from nearby Sanford. "I'll have to pull for Dale Jr. now."

Broken lap belt

As the racing world tried to cope with its grief, investigators were working to find the cause of the fatal crash. Less than a week after the accident, the racing world was further stunned when it was learned that Earnhardt's seat belt broke, which might have contributed to the injuries that killed him, NASCAR officials said.

Earnhardt officially died of a skull fracture when his car crashed into the fourth turn wall on the final lap.

"Our investigation indicates there ➜

DALE EARNHARDT • DALE E.

Brandon Bissell (left) is comforted by Tammy Morgan at a memorial service at the Braun Everiss Wagley Funeral Home in Adrian, Michigan.

NHARDT • DALE EARNHARDT

Helton said the broken left seat belt was discovered during an investigation of Earnhardt's wrecked Chevrolet on Sunday night following the crash.

was a broken left lap belt — the seat belt on the left came apart," said NASCAR president Mike Helton. "We don't know why, we don't know how, we don't know when it broke. We aren't going to speculate today on theories, we aren't going to address any judgment or speculation. We will continue our investigation. We will do our best to come up with as many answers as possible."

Helton said all NASCAR Busch Series and Winston Cup crew chiefs have been informed of the problem in an attempt to correct any faulty seat belts in their cars.

According to Sports Ticker, Helton said the broken left seat belt was discovered during an investigation of Earnhardt's wrecked Chevrolet on Sunday night following the crash. The webbing that goes into the metal buckle broke, according to NASCAR Winston Cup director Gary Nelson. The buckle remained latched, but the belt itself was separated from the metal latches.

Dr. Steve Bohannon, the Daytona International Speedway medical director, explained how the broken seat belt launched Earnhardt's body forward, making it possible for his head to hit other parts inside the race car.

"It appears this allowed his body to move forward and it appears that probably his chin struck the steering column in such a way that the forces were transmitted up the mandible (lower jaw) on each side to fracture the base of his skull," Bohannon said. "Of course, the chest hitting would account for the rib fractures on his left side. He would have had a much better chance to survive if the belt had not broken."

The seat belts were manufactured by Simpson Performance Products. Bill Simpson, the founder and chairman of the company, stands by his products

PHOTOS BY ICON SMI

Investigators have indicated that Earnhardt's lap belt came apart at some point during the crash at Daytona.

DALE EARNHARDT • DALE EA

and issued a release on Friday, February 23, stating that the company has never had a problem in the 43 years of business and "when installed properly," the belt will not fail.

"It is very distressing to lose a good friend and great competitor like Dale Earnhardt," Simpson said in a statement. "It was also distressing to hear this morning that a seat belt that we produced came apart during his fatal crash."

In addition to Earnhardt's fractured skull that killed him, he also suffered broken ribs, broken sternum and a fractured left ankle.

"It appears the major impact for Mr. Earnhardt was forward and to the right,"

Bohannon said. "The belt gave way, which allowed his body to move forward and to the right at which time he more than likely contacted the steering wheel with his chest and his face."

Helton stopped short of laying the responsibility of the material of the belt breaking on the manufacturer or the preparation of the race car, said Sports Ticker.

"We are not going to address any specifics right now," Helton said. "It goes back to jumping to judgments or conclusions that are not founded yet so we are not going to talk about the manufacturers names or anything like that.

"We know more than you do right now, but we are still looking for

answers. We have gone through an extensive period of investigation in this car as we did others in the past. But this one throws a unique angle in it in the fact there is something in that harmonious cocoon that came apart."

Nelson ruled out that the safety workers who tried to extricate Earnhardt's body from the car cut the belts.

"We've never seen it and we have talked to people who are in the business to produce lap belts who have told us they have never seen it," Nelson said. "So in the 52 years of NASCAR Winston Cup racing, this is the first one of these we have seen."

According to Richard Childress, Earnhardt's team owner, the driver wore ➜

The Final Farewell

Helton said NASCAR will seek opinions from garage personnel as to how to improve safety and will also seek advice from outside consultants.

the 5-point seat harness which is the safest restraining system currently used.

However, he was one of just two drivers — Dale Earnhardt Jr. the other — who uses the open-face helmet rather than full-face.

"Dale Earnhardt was one of the most safety conscious drivers out there," Childress said. "We are always looking at safer ways to make these Winston Cup cars. We don't know what to do until the investigation is further down the road. We will run the same stuff here until we know something different."

Helton urged that all competitors

in the Winston Cup and Busch Series garage area will be informed of the potential problem with the seat belt to make sure it doesn't happen again.

"Without any further conclusions to whys, whens and hows, we want to make sure every crew chief in the two garages here this weekend know what we have found," Helton said.

Helton said NASCAR will seek opinions from garage personnel as to how to improve safety and will also seek advice from outside consultants.

As far as any major safety-related changes, such as requiring all drivers to use the Head and Neck Support (HANS) device or installing softer walls, NASCAR officials are not prepared to do that immediately.

"If we knew there was something that we could do, we would do it," Helton said. "In as much that all we know at this point is we have a separated lap belt, that in the 52-year-history of this sport and the industry that developed the pieces, that has never been seen before, we don't have the conclusion today that gives us the ability to react to it."

About changes for the February 25 Dura-Lube 400 at Rockingham, Hilton said, "We aren't going to put up soft ➔

AP/WIDE WORLD PHOTO

Earnhardt Jr. suffered a crash in his first lap of the Dura Lube 400 in Rockingham.

DALE EARNHARDT • DALE E.

Earnhardt's death has increased the focus of safety in auto racing and NASCAR.

PHOTO BY ICON SMI

NHARDT • DALE EARNHARDT

The Final Farewell

"I miss my father and I've cried for him out of my own selfish pity," Earnhardt Jr. said in his first extended comments since his father was killed.

walls, we aren't making any changes unless we find something in the 24 hours that we can specifically do that is a fix and not a detriment to a different area."

The discovery of a broken seat belt in the wreckage of Earnhardt's car seems to explain at least some of the driver's

injuries, according to medical reports.

But some experts argued that a failed seat belt may not account for the skull injury that was Earnhardt's main cause of death.

"I'm not sure what difference [a broken seat belt] made," said Dr. Patrick Lantz, medical examiner for Forsyth County and one of three experts who reviewed Earnhardt's autopsy report.

The idea that the seat-belt break was responsible for Earnhardt's death was advanced by Dr. Bohannon. The theory, said Bohannon, is consistent with measurements of the driver, the car's cockpit and how he hit his chin on the steering wheel.

"[But] this is only one theory," he said.

Junior steps forward

Whatever the cause, nothing will bring the racer back. But the Earnhardt name and tradition will continue with his son. Now that he's had time to ponder the enormity of his loss, Dale Earnhardt Jr. is determined to keep his father's legacy alive.

Earnhardt's death has turned his son, also known as "Little E," into a man — the kind his father had been trying to mold.

"I miss my father and I've cried for him out of my own selfish pity," Earnhardt Jr. told the AP on February 23, in his first extended comments since his father was killed. "But I'm just trying to maintain a good focus for the future and remember that he's in a better place that we all want to be."

Said the AP, "With his red baseball cap on backward and wearing his trendy clothes, Little E still looked like the hotshot rookie who burst onto the NASCAR scene last season. But behind that exterior, it was clear he's grown up."

"You'd probably find that Junior's maturity level has escalated a great deal over the last week," said Larry McReynolds, Earnhardt's former crew chief. "You'll now find him to be a man on a mission to go out and win races, to run for championships, and to be everything his father always hoped for."

The 26-year-old Earnhardt Jr. will try to fill his father's void through his own accomplishments on the racetrack. Besides trying to achieve the same success, he's now charged with overseeing the thriving stable of Winston Cup cars at Dale Earnhardt Inc.

"The three Winston Cup teams — driven by Earnhardt Jr., Steve Park and Daytona winner Michael Waltrip — are

DALE EARNHARDT • DALE E.

Earnhardt Jr. (above and opposite page) has made some lifestyle changes since a recent conversation with his father.

expected to compete for championships for years to come. It's up to him to keep that going," said the AP.

"We've had to take some very deep breaths and get everything in perspective, and it's really been a difficult time," Earnhardt Jr. said. "The main focus now is to try to maintain and progress with the vision my father had with Dale Earnhardt Inc."

Presiding over the late racer's empire is a big job for a young man who up to this point has acquired a reputation for his hard partying and hip, Gen-X good looks. At his father's urging, he had been trying to move away from that image after experiencing his share of losses last season as a rookie driver for DEI.

He won two races, at Richmond and Texas, then won The Winston, NASCAR's all-star race. But things quickly got out of control. His ego got too big, reportedly, and his team noticed. He partied too much and he told too many people about it. His intensely private father stood back and tried to let his son learn his own lessons, but when he thought Junior crossed the line, telling the media about his wild parties in the basement he'd turned into "Club E," the elder Earnhardt intervened.

"My dad said I probably shouldn't have said anything about the nightclub, and at first I didn't think it was a big deal," Earnhardt Jr. said last October. "I let reporters come over to do stories and camera crews in, and after a while I was like, 'Dad's right, what am I doing? This is my house.' "

The talk sparked a change in lifestyle, Earnhardt Jr. has said. He toned down his image and recently talked about wanting to focus only on racing.

Now he is responsible for a multi-

million dollar empire.

"There's been a lot of questions and things running around in our minds," he said. "But the main thing now is to maintain and carry on with the racing program and to try to stick by Teresa the best we can."

A Chilling replay

History came tragically close to repeating itself at the Dura Lube 400 in Rockingham. The horrified audience witnessed another Earnhardt crash. This one walked away.

In a wreck frighteningly similar to the one that killed his father last week, Earnhardt Jr. slammed into the wall on the first lap of the race. He was bruised but fortunately not seriously injured, limping away from the accident to an ambulance that immediately took him to the track medical center. ➜

NHARDT • DALE EARNHARDT

The Final Farewell

Earnhardt Jr. said he had been looking forward to racing again after the long week since his father was killed. It took just one lap to end those plans.

"Somebody got into me," Earnhardt Jr. told his team over the radio. "I was really ready to go racing. We'll be all right, guys."

On a rainy day, when his late father was again the center of attention, Dale Jr. was tapped from behind and slammed into the wall between turns 3 and 4 shortly after a moment of silence to remember The Intimidator. In his second full season driving on the Winston Cup circuit, Earnhardt Jr. started 25th in the 43-car field. The race was delayed 1 hour, 33 minutes by rain, and later was postponed until 11 a.m. the following day because of the weather.

Drivers completed 52 of 393 laps. While his father lost his life in the final lap, Earnhardt Jr. wrecked on the first lap, stunning the 60,000 onlookers and the nationally televised audience watching the race. He was in a tightly bunched pack of cars heading into the third turn on the 1.017-mile North Carolina Speedway oval or "The Rock" as it's known. Robby Gordon swerved down the banked track in front of Earnhardt Jr., who slowed slightly.

Rookie Ron Hornaday Jr. then bumped the rear of Earnhardt's Chevrolet, sending it into the car driven by Kenny Wallace and into the concrete wall at an angle. Earnhardt Jr. was racing at about 150 mph when he crashed.

Asked if he was injured, he smiled and said, "The lap belt was a little too tight. So, I'm a little bruised-up. I'll be OK."

In all, six drivers were involved in Sunday's wreck, including Jimmy Spencer, Mike Wallace and Hut Stricklin. "It was just like a traffic jam," Kenny Wallace said. "Everybody was wanting the bottom of the racetrack and somebody got into the back of Earnhardt and got it starting. It was a bad deal." His brother Mike said, "It's a shame. I thought we were going to be patient, but I guess it wasn't meant to be today."

Earnhardt Jr. said he had been looking forward to racing again after the long week since his father was killed. It took just one lap to end those plans. "I guess we'll just have to wait and get ready to go racing next week in Las Vegas," he said. Before the crash, a pre-race ceremony honored the elder Earnhardt as one of the greatest stock-car racers in history.

As a tribute, most of the drivers and crewmen wore black, red and ➜

AP/WIDE WORLD PHOTOS

Earnhardt Jr. was bruised but not badly injured at Rockingham.

DALE EARNHARDT • DALE E.

INTIMIDATOR

LAST

LAP

500

feb. 18 2001

Greg Dowden of Safety Harbor, Florida, shows off his new tattoo, a tribute to his hero.

The
Final
Farewell

Earnhardt's memory was very much evident at the track with signs and banners honoring him scattered throughout the grandstands and around the grounds of the speedway.

silver caps with Earnhardt's No. 3 on the front. The members of the Dale Earnhardt Inc. team stood on the pit wall during the national anthem holding the caps aloft in a salute to their former boss.

"There's a lot of people here wanting to honor Dale," Jeff Gordon said. "We wanted to put these hats on as a little tribute, to let him know everyone's thinking about him and wishing he was here."

Darrell Waltrip, a retired three-time champion and a longtime friend, asked the spectators to stand and observe a moment of silence, then said a brief prayer. "You wonder how can we go out and race today? We do it knowing

Dale would want us to," Waltrip said.

Earnhardt's memory was very much evident at the track with signs and banners honoring him scattered throughout the grandstands and around the grounds of the speedway. Many in the crowd wore hats, shirts or jackets emblazoned with the No. 3.

There wasn't much racing once the accident was cleaned up. A light rain began during that caution and kept the cars running under a yellow flag until lap 32. Pole-winner Gordon kept the lead until lap 44, when Park moved past to a giant roar from the crowd. Moments later, rain began again and the leaders pitted, leaving Stacy Compton out front. But the rain that began as a sprinkle turned into a downpour that brought out a red flag.

After a 20-minute wait, NASCAR postponed the rest of the race.

Another win for Earnhardt Inc.

With tears in his eyes, Park honored his late boss by driving a Dale Earnhardt car to victory the following day. Park held off Winston Cup champion Bobby Labonte by two car-lengths in the rain-delayed race at North Carolina Speedway.

The scene at Rockingham (above and opposite page) was part memorial, part race.

DALE EARNHARDT • DALE E.

On this day, the sun was shining, and Earnhardt fans had reason to smile again.

"I'm just glad it was Bobby behind me," Park said after the second win of his career. "If it wasn't him, we'd probably both have wrecked. It's been a tough week, and this is just a dream finish."

Park, who started next to pole-sitter Gordon on the front row, was a contender throughout the race. With Earnhardt Jr. coming off basically unscathed from the chilling crash the day before, the victory by Park was especially sweet and a fitting tribute to the late Earnhardt.

Joe Gibbs, who owns the cars driven by defending series champion Bobby Labonte and Tony Stewart, told the AP the postponement was tough on everybody.

"You've got to be resilient," the former Washington Redskins coach said. "You've got to be the kind of team that can bounce back, get ready to go tomorrow and, hopefully, have a good day."

A hometown tribute

On the same day the Dura Lube 400 was originally scheduled, one week after Earnhardt lost his life, yet another and even larger memorial service took place as fans poured into his hometown baseball stadium.

About 5,000 people, most wearing the black-dominated gear of Earnhardt's racing team, braved a cool evening to attend the service at Fieldcrest Cannon Stadium in Kannapolis.

"He was, and still is, our hometown hero," said Doug Stafford, vice president of Lowe's Motor Speedway about 10 miles away.

Earnhardt's oldest son, Kerry, and the driver's sisters, Cathy Watkins and Kay Snipes, spoke at the ballpark service. Snipes, Earnhardt's oldest

sister, read a Bible passage.

"The time of my departure is at hand. I have fought the good fight, I have finished the race, I have kept the faith," she read, quoting the Book of Timothy.

"Tonight we celebrate Dale Earnhardt's life without him," Watkins said. "We're all here together. Family, friends, with tears in our eyes. But we need to wipe those tears away and put smiles on our faces and know that Dale would want us that way. We wanted to say thank you from everyone in our family."

Kerry Earnhardt thanked the crowd for an outpouring of support and prayers for the family and its business. "Keep up the support and concern and the loyalty to Dale Earnhardt Incorporated and NASCAR. We still need you," he said.

In another honor to him, the Class A baseball team that plays on the field was renamed the Intimidators after Earnhardt became a part owner last year.

The final turn

The legend is gone and NASCAR diehards will have to find new heroes to replace Dale Earnhardt behind the wheel.

One reporter maybe summed up the indomitable spirit of NASCAR drivers best when he wrote, "Don't you see? To drivers, the dying is part of the living. It's woven into the thrill, the glory, the sweat. So it figures that when Earnhardt finally gave up the No. 3 car for good on Sunday, they had to cut him out.

"Some guys won't quit any other way."

For Dale Earnhardt, it was always life at full throttle. ∎

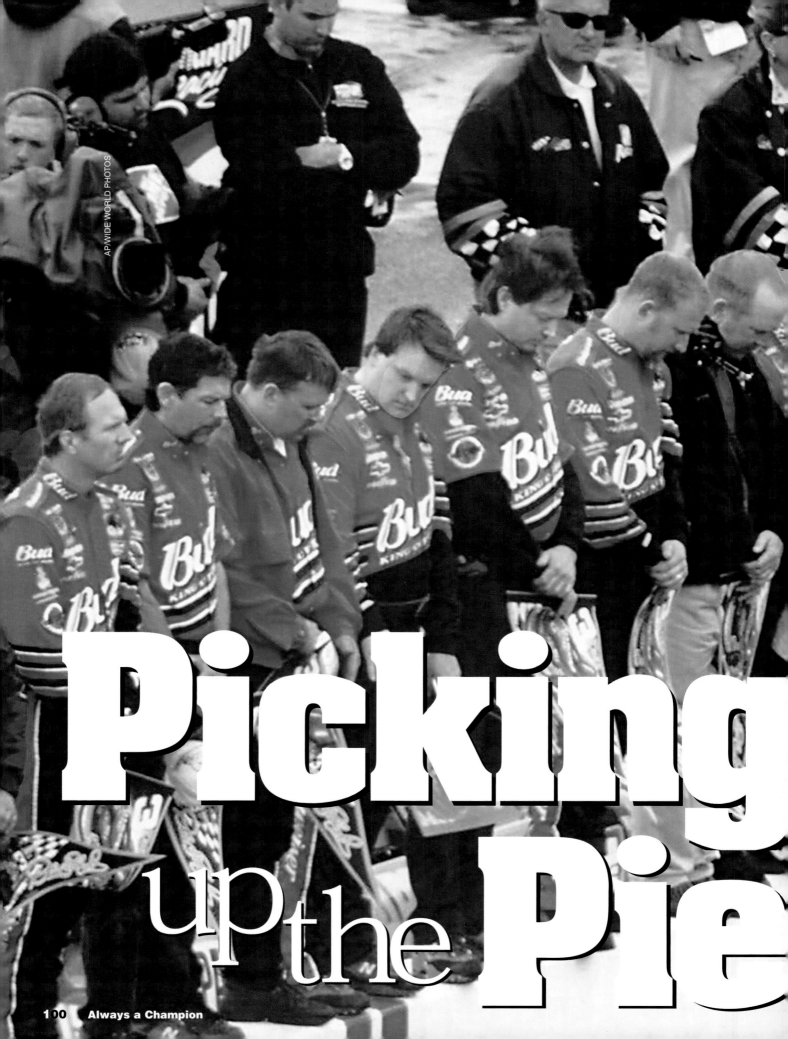

AP/WIDE WORLD PHOTOS

Picking up the Pie

As fans and drivers mourn, NASCAR must find a way to endure without its fallen hero

By Jeff Bartlett

Dale Earnhardt is gone and there is no disputing the fact that he's left behind a gaping hole in the hearts of his fans, which number in the hundreds of thousands. ➜

Picking up the Pieces

Thousands of fans nationwide have left tributes and memorials to the NASCAR legend.

The big questions facing NASCAR in the wake of Earnhardt's death from his crash on the last lap of the 2001 Dayton 500 are these: Is the void Earnhardt leaves in the middle of the sport too wide to be bridged by the current crop of Winston Cup stars? Is Earnhardt's final legacy to be one of improved safety for a racing circuit suddenly besieged by a death to its brightest star?

There is one certainty in the aftermath of Earnhardt's tragic demise, and that is the crushing blow his fans are feeling. "NASCAR has lost the one man who has the biggest and most profound influence on the sport," said fan Dawn Bateman of Columbus, Ohio. "My family and I have been fans of NASCAR, and especially Dale Earnhardt, for many years. Our Sunday afternoons during racing season will never be the same.

"Earnhardt's legacy will live on in the many memories he's given us and the tremendous wealth of knowledge and respect he brought to NASCAR," Bateman continued. "God bless you Dale. We love you and will miss you dearly."

Earnhardt's effect on his following ran so deep that many felt they'd developed personal relationships with The Man in Black without ever having met him. "Dear Dale," one southern race fan wrote as he began a poignant farewell, "you were my Sunday afternoon hero for many years. You were what every arm-chair driver wanted to be. I will miss our race days together because although we never met, you were my friend. You are with our Lord now and need no more prayers, but my family and I will pray for your family to somehow get through this terrible loss. I will always remember you. – Your Friend, Richard Kinkead."

Earnhardt's excellence and never-back-down approach won him some crossover fans who initially cheered against the No. 3 Goodwrench Chevy.

"In the years that I have followed NASCAR racing, Dale Earnhardt has been a powerful force in the sport," said Scott Simpson of West Bloomfield, Michigan. "What started as total frustration with him when he dominated the Fords became immense respect as I watched him fight back with dignity and grace."

The Intimidator built his burgeoning fan base over a long period of years, but he also appealed to those who were new to the sport.

"Our deepest sympathies and regrets go out to the Earnhardt family," wrote the Shatneys of Cornish Flat, New Hampshire. "We have recently become Winston Cup fans and, while not too familiar with Dale's 'Intimidator' tactics, we soon learned that Dale Earnhardt was a force to be reckoned with, and respected.

"He made the sport exciting and action-packed," the Shatneys added. "He always gave his best to the fans and to the sport. He was, and shall always be, a legend in the eyes of

the NASCAR world. The tracks of Winston Cup racing will always seem to be missing something without the black 3 out there to keep the other drivers on their toes."

Fellow drivers mourn

The loss of Earnhardt, who won 76 Winston Cup races and seven different points championships, also had a profound effect on his fellow Winston Cup drivers. Jeff Gordon won the pole for the Dura Lube 400 and then entered the media center at North Carolina Speedway for his post-qualifying press conference wearing a No. 3 cap in honor of Earnhardt.

"I put this hat on to let everybody know we're thinking of Dale," Gordon said. "I want to dedicate this pole to him. It's a great opportunity

to let everybody know how much I respected him and how much we're going to miss him. Brooke [Gordon's wife] and I are deeply saddened by this devastating loss. Not only is it a huge loss for this sport, but a huge loss for me personally. Dale taught me so much and became a great friend."

Dale Jarrett expressed a common sentiment among the drivers when he explained how he lost far more than just a fellow competitor, but also a buddy.

"The sport and the race that he truly loved has taken from me one of my best friends," said Jarrett. "I know I should feel fortunate that I had the opportunity to race with, tangle with, sometimes outrun and most usually finish behind the greatest driving talent NASCAR has ever seen. ➔

Gordon wears his tribute hat at the Dura Lube 400.

Picking up the Pieces

"I am thankful for that opportunity, but more importantly, I am most grateful that I had the chance to know Dale Earnhardt in a way that so many people could only dream of. He was a true friend. I looked up to him not only for his driving skill, but because he was so much more to so many people, including my family."

Jimmy Spencer also revealed the softer side of Earnhardt. "I can't believe Dale Earnhardt isn't with us anymore and that he's not going to be out there every week in that black Number 3," he said. "There isn't anyone I loved racing more against than him because he was the best, and you always want to challenge yourself against the best.

"The thing about Dale Earnhardt," Spencer explained, "is that there were two Dale Earnhardts — the Dale Earnhardt that raced you for every inch of the track and the Dale Earnhardt who cared about making people happy.

"He loved my mom and dad. Every time he saw me at the track he'd ask how my mom and dad were doing. Every time he saw my mom he grabbed her hand and would stop and talk for a minute. He did it just last week at Daytona.

"I'll miss him. I was talking to my dad today, and I said to him, 'What are we gonna do as drivers?' We all congregated around him. I don't care if you were Rusty Wallace or Dale Jarrett or who it was, we all talked to him because he was the guy."

Passing the torch

Indeed, what will the Winston Cup drivers do now? Who is going to step forward and pick up the slack for a sport that is sure to take a hit without Earnhardt and the No. 3 car around? Who will step up and be "The Guy?" Winston Cup officials would sure like to know.

Gordon is an obvious choice because of the big fan base he's built during his speedy run to Winston Cup stardom. But Gordon, as one fan insisted, does not come from true NASCAR stock because of California and Indiana roots.

Jarrett, defending Winston Cup points champ Bobby Labonte, Rusty Wallace, Tony Stewart or Jeff Burton may be capable of filling the void. But Jarrett may be too nice, Labonte too laid back, Wallace is waning, Stewart is currently far too temperamental and Burton needs to win some big ones.

So the perfect choice to succeed Dale Earnhardt Sr. as the Winston Cup torchbearer is Dale Earnhardt Jr. He has the same North Carolina NASCAR roots, and he already has huge fan support.

Following back-to-back Busch Grand National points championships, Dale Jr. enjoyed a fledgling Winston Cup season in which he won two races and The Winston, and wound up just 30 points shy of beating Matt Kenseth for Rookie of the Year honors.

His pedigree is unquestioned, and his popularity has zoomed since he climbed into the No. 8 Budweiser Chevrolet. The loss of Dale Sr. could have a hugely negative impact on Winston Cup unless someone rises up to the mantle. It's a weighty burden, but Little E seems to be maturing to the task.

"We've really had to take some very deep breaths and get everything in perspective, and it's been a really tough time," said Earnhardt Jr., who inherited the massive Dale Earnhardt Inc. stable far sooner than he ever imagined. "The main focus now is to try to maintain the progress and the vision my father had with Dale Earnhardt Inc."

Sticking to their guns

Of course, much of the recent focus has centered around safety. Could the new HANS (Head and Neck Support) device have saved Dale Earnhardt? Did his safety belt break because of the severity of his head-on impact with the wall?

Most of the drivers are dismissing the bulky U-shaped HANS device — which is designed to keep a driver's head and neck more stable during the rapid deceleration that occurs in a head-on collision — until further testing.

"I don't feel like all of a sudden, just because of what happened to Dale, I need to run with it," Gordon said. "The HANS is the best device we have to date, but I'm not saying it's the best thing. I'm still testing it and trying to make it work, but I don't have it in my car at this time."

Veteran Mark Martin was even more emphatic. "I won't wear one of those devices for anything," he insisted. "I can tell just by looking at it I wouldn't wear it. It's just not for me and I'm not even going to tinker with it." →

Fans lament the loss of their hero outside Daytona USA in Daytona Beach.

Picking up the Pieces

Another fallen hero

Clearly, though, something needs to be done, whether it's the HANS, an improvement in the safety belt harness that some experts say broke and caused Earnhardt to suffer a greater impact than normal, or perhaps softening the concrete walls with some kind of overlay. NASCAR fans are growing weary of watching their heroes die.

"If anybody else gets killed, I'm never going to another race again because I can't take much more of it," said Pam Solomon of Kannapolis, North Carolina, Earnhardt's hometown. "I haven't gotten over Kenny [Irwin] yet, and now Dale. I mean, this is devastating for race fans."

Alan Norman of Bedford, Indiana, perhaps summed up the sentiments best with his reaction to the passing of his hero.

"The racing world and my son and my family have lost the greatest race-car driver that ever lived," he said. "I have never had such a feeling of loss in my life from someone I never got to meet. There wasn't a day that would go by that I didn't think about or talk about Dale.

"Race day won't be the same without him. You either loved him or you hated him, but I truly loved the man and the way he drove that black Number 3." ∎

Brian Lawrence comforts Susan Adcock outside the North Carolina Speedway.

Earnhardt Jr. prepares for the start of the Dura Lube 400 at Rockingham, North Carolina.

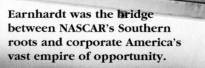

Earnhardt was the bridge between NASCAR's Southern roots and corporate America's vast empire of opportunity.

A

Da

Modern Day Hero

Earnhardt stands tall among those who shaped their sports

By Jason Wilde

Michael Waltrip was waiting. Waiting for the man who had hired him despite the fact that Waltrip had never won a Winston Cup race before, in 462 tries. Waiting for the man who helped seal off the competition behind him so he could win the 2001 Daytona 500. Waiting for the one man who would make his first Victory Lane celebration complete. Waiting for Dale Earnhardt. ➜

A Modern Day Hero

"I had won the race and I was telling everybody about it, and I just couldn't wait until I got that big grab on the neck, that big hug," Waltrip said. "I just knew any minute, Dale was going to run into Victory Lane and say, 'That's what I'm talking about, right there.' But that wasn't to be."

Sadly, it was not meant to be. Earnhardt, Waltrip's car owner and a seven-time Winston Cup champion, was dead, killed instantly from massive head injures sustained in a crash in the final turn of the final lap of the race.

In the aftermath of Earnhardt's death, news reports focused on the facts that Earnhardt wore an old-fashioned open-faced helmet and chose not to use some of NASCAR's other basic safety innovations, such as the Head And Neck Support (HANS) brace that recently has been touted as a way to prevent serious head injuries. Later, it was learned that Earnhardt's seat belt was broken when he crashed, apparently causing the legendary driver's head to slam into the steering wheel and killing him instantly. According to a report in the *New York Daily News*, Earnhardt altered the seat belt before the race, possibly playing a hand in his death.

Whatever the cause of Earnhardt's tragic death, it leaves the sport with even more questions about its future.

Carrying NASCAR

On February 18, the day Earnhardt died, the Daytona 500 broke television-ratings records on FOX. It was the first race of NASCAR's new six-year, $2.4 billion television contract with Fox, NBC and Turner Sports, which promised to increase the sport's national exposure. Fox's rating for Sunday's Daytona 500 was the highest in 15 years and 11 percent better than what CBS did on last year's race. And it could easily be argued that the deal never would have happened without him. And now, that's exactly what NASCAR is faced with — life without Dale Earnhardt.

"He was a good friend, and I'm still in shock. This is a terrible, terrible loss," said Humpy Wheeler, president of Lowe's Motor Speedway in Charlotte. "For me, it ranks right up there with the death of JFK. Dale was the Michael Jordan of our sport. We always thought of Dale as being invincible. So when he didn't climb out of that car after the wreck, I knew it was bad.

"We've lost our Michael Jordan," Wheeler surmised. "We not only lost a great driver, but we lost one of America's real sports heroes. There will never be anybody like him again. He was a throwback to the drivers that made this sport. He was tough and he gave it all he had every time that he ran. This

Now Earnhardt Jr. (right) may be charged with carrying the heaviest torch in racing.

just leaves a terrible hole, a terrible black hole."

The loss of Earnhardt — the sport's most recognizable driver, biggest draw and most bankable commodity — is the fourth NASCAR death since the start of the 2000 season. And because of his stature in the sport, it could prove devastating. While Earnhardt left behind a family — including his third wife, Teresa; his youngest of four children, 12-year-old daughter Taylor; and his namesake, 26-year-old driver Dale Earnhardt Jr. — he also left behind a void in the sport he had in large part delivered from its regional roots in the South into a national pastime.

Where will stock-car racing go without him? "That's a tough one," said Earnhardt's close friend Richard Childress, who owns the No. 3 car Earnhardt had driven. "I ask where Richard Childress goes without him. I don't know."

"He made us all better drivers because he set a standard of excellence we all aspired to achieve," said driver Tony Stewart.

Rookie Kevin Harvick will fill Earnhardt's seat for the rest of the season. But he knows he will never be able to replace the legend, The Intimidator. "Dale Earnhardt was probably the best race driver there will ever be in NASCAR," said Harvick, whose Chevrolet was painted white and re-numbered No. 29 for the race at Rockingham a week after Earnhardt's death. "Nobody will ever replace him."

Yet somehow the sport must go on. The scheduled race at Rockingham was delayed a day by rain, but it wasn't cancelled. Earnhardt Jr. said he never seriously thought about not racing a week after his father's death. As hard as it was, the show went on. But it wasn't the same.

The comparisons of Earnhardt to Tiger Woods, well on his way to becoming the greatest player in the history of golf, and to Michael Jordan, the former Chicago Bulls star who transcended the sport of basketball to become the best-known athlete in history, are fitting. Jordan wasn't only a scoring champion and the leader of the Bulls' six NBA championship teams, he was an entertainer who became the sport's ambassador, spokesman and most popular figure. Woods took a sport that had been largely a country-club, white-dominated endeavor and popularized it across economic, social and racial lines.

Like other all-time greats, Earnhardt's legacy extends well beyond his sport, and those outside ➜

The Intimidator meant as much or more to auto racing as Michael Jordan did to basketball.

A Modern Day Hero

NASCAR's scope are feeling the brunt of his loss. Much like the post-Jordan NBA, which is still reeling in the wake of his 1998 retirement, the NASCAR circuit faces an unknown future without its biggest star.

And, as Winston Cup's biggest hero and biggest villain, Earnhardt gave everyone something to cheer about — for him or against him.

Although there are certainly fans who grew tired of Jordan's and Woods' success, and those who may delight in Woods' recent winless streak or Jordan's struggles as general manager of the lowly Washington Wizards, neither athlete could inspire the divisiveness of Earnhardt. Love him or hate him, you couldn't ignore him. You may have cheered for Jeff Gordon or Dale Jarrett or Mark Martin instead, but however reluctantly, you knew that Earnhardt was one of a kind. If you bought a ticket or turned on the television, you did so at least partially because you wanted to see what would happen to The Man in Black.

Unprecedented influence

And yet, it's not a foregone conclusion that Earnhardt was the greatest racer in NASCAR history. Richard Petty, the all-time victory leader with 200 career wins, captured more checkered flags than than Earnhardt (76). So did David Pearson, Darrell Waltrip, Bobby Allison and Cale Yarborough. And while Earnhardt dominated his era and was a colorful character, stock-car racing has always had colorful characters and dominant drivers.

Petty, for example, was the first NASCAR driver whose fame transcended the sport. His 200 wins will probably never be repeated. His nickname was "The King."

The difference, NASCAR experts say,

was the timing of Earnhardt's run to greatness. It coincided perfectly with and played a vital role in the sport's boom in popularity, which took NASCAR out of the South and into America's living rooms. The sport grew exponentially during Earnhardt's career.

For NASCAR, his rise came just in time, because Petty, Pearson, Allison and Yarborough were nearing the end of their careers. And he came along just as television embraced NASCAR. In his rookie year, CBS ran the first start-to-finish coverage of the Daytona 500. By the early 1990s, all of the races were televised live.

"He took the sport to new places," said former driver Ned Jarrett, now a television commentator. "He leaves a big, big void that will be very hard to fill."

In Earnhardt, racing also found a spokesman, one who was vital to the sport's growing appeal among corporate sponsors. Atlanta-based NAPA, for example, became a sponsor of Waltrip after a personal appeal from Earnhardt. Coca-Cola, the official soft drink of NASCAR, featured Earnhardt in promotions. Go into your local K-Mart, and you'll probably find an Oreo display with Earnhardt's mustachioed smiling face, getting ready to munch on the chocolaty sandwich cookie. It has become common for consumer-oriented companies to sign on as NASCAR sponsors, but it was Earnhardt, who drove for Wrangler jeans in the early 1980s, who helped make racing more attractive to mainstream companies.

"His influence was phenomenal," Steve Handschuh, president of NAPA auto parts stores, told *The Atlanta Journal-Constitution*. "Dale Earnhardt did more to fuel the explosive growth of NASCAR than any other driver."

"He was somebody who made the

transition and was a bridge from the old NASCAR stereotype of the guy running moonshine to the corporate world of today," Carol Schumacher, a spokeswoman for Home Depot, told the Atlanta newspaper.

Not only that, but Earnhardt accounted for an estimated 40 to 50 percent of the memorabilia sold at NASCAR races and was responsible for six percent of Speedway's $317 million in total revenue. His Intimidator moniker sold T-shirts and caps faster than all the other drivers combined. Only Jordan has sold more merchandise, according to *Forbes* magazine.

"He may have only had a ninth-grade education, but he was a genius," said Don Hawk, Earnhardt's former business manager. Earnhardt's off-the-track financial empire is worth an estimated $20-to-25 million a year, and his business endeavors ranged from a car dealership to a minor-league baseball team.

On the first day of trading after Earnhardt's death, shares of Speedway Motorsports Inc. fell $1.24 to $24.04. According to a report in *The Raleigh News & Observer*, Speedway may have to suspend plans to sell lucrative naming rights to its tracks. Meanwhile, shares fell 88 cents to $41.63 for International Speedway Corp, which owns the Daytona International Speedway where Earnhardt crashed.

All told, Earnhardt's financial, social and competitive impact on racing will probably never be equaled by any driver, in any era. "It's going to take time," former NASCAR president Bill France said of the sport's ability to recover from the devastating loss.

It may just take a long, long time. ■

"He was somebody who made the transition and was the bridge from the old NASCAR stereotype of the guy running moonshine to the corporate world of today."

– Steve Handschuh,
NAPA President

On a Roll

Dominant for the better part of two decades, Earnhardt didn't have to rely on luck for his seven Winston Cup titles

By Aaron George

hough it's impossible to quantify the greatness of the most influential and groundbreaking driver in the history of NASCAR, Dale Earnhardt's seven Winston Cup championships are as close to a measuring stick as you'll find. When fans and historians consider all the races he won and all the pressures he overcame to capture those coveted titles, it's easy to see why he's considered to be at least an equal to the legendary Richard Petty, the man with whom he shares the record for most Winston Cup championships. So here's a salute to The Intimidator and his remarkable run, as we highlight each of those seven magical seasons.

1980
1986
1987
1990
1991
1993
1994

nston Cup

On a Roll

Championship Season Statistics

1980	
Starts	31
Wins	5
Top-5 Finishes	19
Top-10 Finishes	24
Crew Chiefs	Jake Elder, Doug Richert
Car Owner	Rod Osturlund
Car Makes	Chevrolet Monte Carlo, Olds Cutlass
Car Number	2
Primary Sponsor	Mike Curb Productions

The First Run to Greatness

Few expected a driver just one year removed from his rookie season to contend for NASCAR's crown jewel, much less win it. But Earnhardt quickly served notice that his 1979 Rookie of the Year performance was no fluke, as he out-raced legends Cale Yarborough and Petty on the path to his first Winston Cup Series title.

Eager to prove his worth to team owner Rod Osturlund, who had given him a chance on the NASCAR circuit a year earlier, Earnhardt won five races and posted an incredible 24 top-10 finishes. Earnhardt's No. 2 Monte Carlo found itself in the winner's circle after key showdowns at Atlanta (his first career superspeedway victory), Bristol and his home track of Charlotte.

Yarborough's competitive spirit kept the title in doubt to the very end. But The Intimidator's fifth-place showing at California secured him just enough points to become the only driver to claim the Winston Cup title one year after winning Rookie of the Year. →

AP/WIDE WORLD PHOTO

1980

Earnhardt won five races and posted an incredible 24 top-10 finishes.

On a Roll

1986	
Starts	29
Wins	5
Top-5 Finishes	16
Top-10 Finishes	23
Crew Chief	Kirk Shelmerdine
Car Owner	Richard Childress
Car Make	Chevrolet Monte Carlo
Car Number	3
Primary Sponsor	Wrangler

Back Where He Belongs

Now competing for Richard Childress Racing, Earnhardt battled his way back to the top after finishing eighth or better in the points standings four of the previous five years. But his second championship would not come easily.

Darrell Waltrip gained an early season points lead and appeared invincible until the pivotal race in Richmond, where The Intimidator validated his nickname. Waltrip tried to overtake Earnhardt for the lead with just three laps remaining, but Earnhardt met his attempt with a hearty bump on the third turn, resulting in a four-car accident. The Intimidator's tactic worked, as he was fined $3,000 for "reckless driving" but finished the race in third compared to Waltrip's fifth.

That bold move set up Earnhardt's win in Atlanta, where he led all but three of the final 138 laps and essentially wrapped up the season victory. It would be the first time since 1978 that the championship was clinched before the year's final race. Earnhardt's $1.7 million in winnings set a new mark for one year. ➜

Rival Waltrip was overtaken at the pivotal race in Richmond.

Winston Cup

1986

Earnhardt battled his way back to the top after finishing eighth or better in the points standings four of the previous five years.

On a Roll

1987	
Starts	29
Wins	11
Top-5 Finishes	21
Top-10 Finishes	24
Crew Chief	Kirk Shelmerdine
Car Owner	Richard Childress
Car Make	Chevrolet Monte Carlo
Car Number	3
Primary Sponsor	Wrangler

No Signs of Slowing

Earnhardt was now firmly established as a superstar of his sport, but that wasn't good enough. The Intimidator sought utter domination, and got it, in the form of 11 victories and 21 top-five finishes in 29 starts. His unfathomable streak began with a win at Rockingham, followed by more of the same at Richmond, Darlington, North Wilkesboro, Bristol and Martinsville. Earnhardt had six triumphs in the first eight races of 1987.

Working on a new streak that same season, The Intimidator all but clinched the crown at Richmond with his third straight victory (preceded by wins at Bristol and the Southern 500 at Darlington). The win at Richmond gave him an unheard-of 608-point lead over Bill Elliott, his nearest rival. He officially secured the points championship with a second-place showing at Rockingham, which marked the earliest a driver had clinched since Yarborough in 1977. ➜

Elliott and the rest were left fighting for second place.

Winston Cup

1987

The Intimidator sought utter domination, and got it, in the form of 11 victories and 21 top-five finishes in 29 starts.

On a Roll

1990	
Starts	29
Wins	9
Top-5 Finishes	18
Top-10 Finishes	23
Crew Chief	Kirk Shelmerdine
Car Owner	Richard Childress
Car Make	Chevrolet Lumina
Car Number	3
Primary Sponsor	GM Goodwrench

Earning His Keep

Angry over his second-place finish in 1989, Earnhardt approached 1990 with renewed vigor. Competitors felt the brunt of this intensity, which helped him claim nine wins and 18 top-fives. Earnhardt led the points standings heading into the Budweiser 500 at Dover, where an engine breakdown forced him into the garage early in the race. A spirited effort by his crew put his car back on the track just over 90 minutes later, and he was able to pick up 12 points.

Though the effort proved symbolic — he won the title by 24 points — it illustrated the unbreakable resolve of the team and its driver.

Earnhardt's third place at the season finale in Atlanta was enough to best Mark Martin, who waged a serious challenge for the points championship but fell short when he came in sixth. The series win was Earnhardt's first in the now-legendary black Goodwrench Chevrolet, as he set another record by earning $3.3 million for the year. ➜

1990

The series win was Earnhardt's first in the now-legendary black Goodwrench Chevrolet, as he set another record by earning $3.3 million for the year.

On a Roll

1991	
Starts	29
Wins	4
Top-5 Finishes	14
Top-10 Finishes	21
Crew Chief	Kirk Shelmerdine
Car Owner	Richard Childress
Car Make	Chevrolet Lumina
Car Number	3
Primary Sponsor	GM Goodwrench

Repeating Glory ... again

The Intimidator was growing increasingly comfortable behind the wheel of his Chevy Lumina and was poised for even more dominance in '91. And although the win total slipped from nine to four, the team's consistency was evident in the 21 top-10 finishes in 29 total starts.

Displaying unrivaled skills in tight quarters and an unflappabe demeanor, Earnhardt eased to victory at the early season Busch Clash. Even the new inverted format wouldn't derail the indomitable No. 3. He dominated the field during the first 10 laps, then, starting from the back, out-manuevered the 14-car lineup to take the second half of the sprint as well.

Earnhardt's reaction, "It was pretty awesome, wasn't it?," summed up his performance in that race and in the season, as he cruised to a 195-point victory margin in the standings. ➔

AP/WIDE WORLD PHOTO

Winston Cup

1991

Displaying unrivaled skills in tight quarters and an unflappabe demeanor, Earnhardt eased to victory at the early season Busch Clash.

On a Roll

1993	
Starts	30
Wins	6
Top-5 Finishes	17
Top-10 Finishes	21
Crew Chief	Andy Petree
Car Owner	Richard Childress
Car Make	Chevrolet Lumina
Car Number	3
Primary Sponsor	GM Goodwrench

Back in Black

Just when NASCAR drivers were hoping and praying he was over the hill, The Man in Black came roaring back to win his sixth Winston Cup title. Although this season wasn't marked by the domination he demonstrated in other championship runs, Earnhardt found a way to win. The Intimidator's four victories were enough, as his trademark consistency resulted in 17 top-five finishes and 21 in the top 10 — good for an 80-point triumph over rival competitor Rusty Wallace.

Besting Wallace in a key head-to-head battle made all the difference. As the two veterans struggled for the lead at the Talladega 400, Wallace was sent flipping through the infield grass. The incident may have unnerved Wallace, as it took several races for him to regain the form that put him in the points lead earlier in the season. The Intimidator gained the upper hand in the standings the very next race at Sears Point and held on for a 10th-place finish — and the points championship — at the season-ending race in Atlanta. ➜

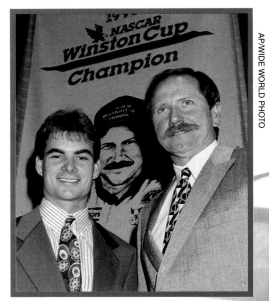

Earnhardt's 17 top fives were too much for Jeff Gordon and company.

AP/WIDE WORLD PHOTO

Winston Cup

1993

Just when NASCAR drivers were hoping and praying he was over the hill, "the man in black" came roaring back to win his sixth Winston Cup title.

On a Roll

1994	
Starts	31
Wins	4
Top-5 Finishes	14
Top-10 Finishes	20
Crew Chief	Andy Petree
Car Owner	Richard Childress
Car Make	Chevrolet Lumina
Car Number	3
Primary Sponsor	GM Goodwrench

One for the Ages

After winning five championships in the last eight years for team-owner Childress, everyone was gunning to derail Earnhardt and his Chevy-Goodwrench freight train. More than two dozen changes were made by other drivers and teams in the off-season, all with the goal of stopping The Intimidator.

All the modifications in the world made little difference, as Earnhardt cruised to yet another Winston Cup championship, tying him with Petty for the all-time mark. Notching four victories and an impressive 20 top-10 finishes gave Earnhardt the milestone.

Earnhardt's 10-year run for the Childress Racing Team was among the most prolific in history. He had garnered more than 50 victories, 32 seconds and 37 third-place finishes.

By 1994, Dale Earnhardt had accumulated more earnings competing for Childress than any other driver had won in a career. ■

AP/WIDE WORLD PHOTO

Winston Cup

1994

All the modifications in the world made little difference, as Earnhardt cruised to yet another Winston Cup championship.

PHOTO BY ICON SMI

The Man in Black

in

By Benjamin Roberts

Gatorade
125's

Earnhardt somehow seemed destined for racing greatness

umbers…BIG numbers. Seven Winston Cup points championships. Six-hundred seventy-six career races. Seventy-six career Winston Cup race victories. Four-hundred twenty top-10 finishes. But in the world of stock car racing all of those numbers — impressive as they may be — pale in comparison to a single, simple number: No. 3 — the number on the car of racing super-legend Dale Earnhardt.

Before his tragic death at Daytona International Speedway, "The Intimidator," as he had come to be known, had ascended to the level of sports celebrity, emerging as the top star in racing and one of the best-known personalities in all of sports.

It might seem clichéd to suggest that Dale Earnhardt was destined to achieve the level of stardom that he did, but all the elements for the North Carolina native to succeed were in place almost from the very beginning

The Man in Black

Following in the footsteps

Born in Kannapolis, North Carolina, in 1951, Dale was the son of a racing legend. In fact, Dale's father, Ralph Earnhardt, is often mentioned as one of the pioneers of the modern-day NASCAR circuit. The winner of the 1956 NASCAR Sportsman Championship, Ralph was considered one of the top drivers of the Grand National division — the division that would go on to become the Winston Cup Series.

Respected for his skill, Ralph was renowned for his fiery and competitive spirit, a trait he apparently passed along to his son Dale.

Dale also inherited a dream from his father — a dream to make a living as a race-car driver.

"My earliest memory is of watching daddy in a race," Dale was quoted as saying in 1976. "Following in his footsteps is all I've ever wanted to do."

Ralph relished, and succeeded, when up against the top level of NASCAR drivers in his day, as his 1956 championship indicates. But wary of the extensive travel involved, he opted out of a number of events in the Grand National series. Instead he chose to compete locally, where the farthest jaunt was just a several-hour car ride to places like Richmond or other tracks throughout the Carolinas.

Even though his racing concentrated primarily in the hotbeds of the Carolinas and various other East Coast locations, Ralph racked up an astronomical amount of victories, including his 1956 championship run.

"If they kept records of it, Ralph Earnhardt has probably won more races than any other driver in the country," rival and contemporary great Bobby Isaac once said.

Ralph's success in stock-car racing made those footsteps an easier path to trace. The elder Earnhardt kept a garage in the family's backyard, where he would keep his racing vehicles and parts. In addition to the wealth of knowledge and experience he could share with his son, Ralph's garage provided young Dale a physical, hands-on approach few get to engage in so early in life.

"I remember Daddy going racing during the week, and I couldn't wait until I got home from school the next day to find out everything that had happened," Dale said in the Frank Vehorn biography, *The Intimidator*. "I wanted to hear it all. The only things I remember doing much as a kid was helping Daddy with the race cars, doing whatever he'd let me do, and being around racing people. I couldn't wait until I got old enough to drive race cars myself."

By all accounts, Dale had a happy, if not pampered, upbringing in Kannapolis, a cotton-mill town between

Dale's oldest son, Kerry, is a third-generation stock-car racer.

Charlotte and Winston-Salem. He grew up in a modest two-story house along with two brothers, both younger, and two sisters, both older.

"I had a lot of fun growing up," Dale once reflected. "We didn't have all the finer things in life, but we still had a good time. I can't ever remember wanting anything that I didn't already have."

Dale was close with both his father and mother, Martha, although his relationship with them was severely tested when he dropped out of high school in 1966. Unhappy in the classroom and brimming with the desire to focus on his passion, racing, his parents were extremely disappointed with his decision.

A year later, Dale married for the first time and his wife soon gave birth to a boy, Kerry, in 1969. The marriage was not meant to be, however, and ended in divorce. Dale married again, and was the proud father of two more children — Kelly King in 1972 and Ralph Dale Jr., in 1974. Unfortunately, his second marriage also did not last.

Dale bounced around at various jobs after dropping out, including stints at a local service station and at a mill. While satisfied to be making it on his own — by however small a margin — Dale knew he wanted something more. He was mostly working at the mill, which only served to steel his idea to find his break as a race-car driver.

Driving a Ford Falcon, Dale began competing on local short tracks, where he was relatively successful right from the start.

All seemed to be happy for the Earnhardt family. Father and son had patched up their differences over Dale's now admittedly unwise decision to drop out of school. Ralph continued to pay the bills, and Dale was able to make ends meet while still managing to make a go at a racing career of his own.

By most accounts, all was well with the Earnhardts. But, without notice, Dale's world would be turned upside down, due to a family tragedy on September 27, 1973. The day started as so many others did for Dale. He went ➜

The grave site of Ralph Earnhardt, who died unexpectedly in 1973, has received new attention since his son's tragic death in 2001.

The Man in Black

into Ralph's garage, planning to work alongside his father. What he found, though, would change his life forever.

Dale found his father slumped over a car, lifeless. Ralph had suffered a massive heart attack — dead at age 45. Just when it appeared that Dale was going to be able to share his racing career with the man he idolized — the father whose footsteps Dale was intent to follow — it was all taken away from him.

Dale was devastated. "I was so mad at him for leaving this world," he said in Frank Moriarty's biography, *Dale Earnhardt*. "I didn't get over it for a year. I'm still not over it. There isn't a day that goes by that I don't think about my father."

Opportunity cost

Dale struggled ahead following the death of his father. Though he was still aching from the loss, Dale was even more determined than ever to take up after his race car-driving father. Ready to

PHOTOS COURTESY OF DRIVERONAMISSION.COM

focus all of his energies into his dream, Dale quit his job at a wheel alignment shop in Concord, North Carolina, to follow his lifelong ambition. It was a risky move financially, but Dale was certain he was doing the right thing.

Being successful in stock-car racing requires more than talent and skill. It takes speed. And, when it comes to automobiles, money fuels speed. Cars, engines, parts, repairs — none were cheap, but all were needed if Dale was going to make racing his living.

Dale worked out of his father's shop, doing his own maintenance work while competing at dirt track raceways throughout the region. He borrowed money to help finance his fledgling career, hoping to stay afloat by besting the competition.

Dale had little margin for error. A strong performance at the track could possibly net ➔

Top: Dale proudly stands near his car in a late-'70s shot.

Bottom: A youthful Dale at Charlotte Motor Speedway, 1976.

The Man in Black

several thousand dollars, while a string of lackluster ones would threaten economic ruin.

Onto the beaten path

Dale left the dirt-track circuit in 1974, entering NASCAR's Sportsman division, which staged its races on asphalt surfaces. "I was doing good on dirt and I could have made a living from it," Dale said. "But I knew I had to make the switch to get where I wanted to go, which was NASCAR racing."

After purchasing a five-year old Dodge from Harry Gant — another future NASCAR star — Dale entered his first race in the Sportsman division in the World Service Life 300 at the tricky high-banked Charlotte Motor Speedway. He held his own, placing 13th.

But Dale was just getting his first taste of the track in Charlotte. He returned in 1975 to compete in his first Winston Cup race, where he finished 22nd at the World 600 after starting the race at 33rd.

"There was a whole lot of difference driving asphalt, but I was always glad that I started out on dirt," Dale said. "I learned some things that helped me out when I got on the Winston Cup circuit and began racing on the big tracks. You learn the feel of a car and sharpen your reflexes by racing on dirt. It bothers some guys when their cars get loose on the big tracks and they can feel air coming through the side window. But not me."

Few things would bother the indomitable Earnhardt. He continued to make ends meet in the Sportsman division. He did make two Winston Cup starts in 1976, although he dropped out of both races, including an end-over-end wreck in Atlanta.

Still, the two runs brought in about $3,000. He made just one Winston Cup start in 1977. Despite his limited number

PHOTO BY TIMEPIX

of starts, his Sportsman performances were enough to catch the attention of some of the sport's management.

Investing in the future

By no means a runaway success, Dale felt good about his prospects for a pro racing career. While his achievements were still somewhat modest, things seemed to be pointed in the right direction. He was paying his dues on the circuits and gaining valuable experience and training along the way.

But despite his slowly budding career, perhaps the best thing to happen to Dale was his introduction to Teresa Houston. Like Dale, Teresa also came from a North Carolina racing family, and the two quickly hit it off.

With Teresa's background, she was familiar with the racing lifestyle and all that comes along with it — the long hours, extensive traveling and the dangers of the track. Dale and Teresa continued to date, marrying in 1982.

Still, the late '70s weren't always the best of times for Dale. While he was able to continue to build his racing résumé, his funds were nearly exhausted. The high costs of parts, repairs, travel and even gasoline were catching up to him.

"I kept racing, getting deeper and deeper in debt, and really didn't know just how far in debt I was," Dale recalled. "I was asking myself what I should do. I still believed I was going to make it, and a lot of people were trying to help me and were saying they knew I could do it. But my money was gone and I knew I couldn't keep on borrowing and borrowing."

Things got so bad that Dale had reportedly begun to consider selling some of his equipment to help keep the debt collectors at bay. But that's when Dale's big break finally came.

Dale had entered four races in 1978 for owner Will Cronkite, including the Firecracker 400 in Daytona, where Dale earned his first Top 10 finish despite starting in the 28th position. That caught the attention of West Coast businessman Rod Osterlund. Osterlund owned a Winston Cup team — Osterlund Racing — that made its debut on the circuit in 1977. Osterlund had met Dale on several occasions, and after seeing him in his earlier races in 1978, decided he wanted the fiery,

aggressive driver on his team.

After he made an initial run in a Sportsman race at the Charlotte Motor Speedway, Dale got his chance to show his stuff on the Winston Circuit. Impressed with what he saw in the Charlotte race, Osterlund offered Dale the chance to drive a second car for the Osterlund racing team, along with primary driver Dave Marcis.

Finally, Dale had the financing of Osterlund's team to be able to put a first-rate car on the trip — one that was backed up by a NASCAR quality road crew. And Dale didn't disappoint. In his first Winston Cup race for Osterlund at the Atlanta International Speedway, Dale turned in an eye-opening fourth-place finish. Marcis finished just ahead of

Teresa Earnhardt during happier times.

PHOTO BY ICON SMI

Dale in third.

Right from the start, the decision looked like it would be a winner for both Dale and Osterlund.

Two weeks later, Dale raced again for the Osterlund team, competing in a season-ending event at the Ontario Motor Speedway outside of Los Angeles. Dale finished 11th, especially impressive considering it was his first time at the California raceway.

Meanwhile, Marcis was feuding with Osterlund team manager Roland Wlodyka, and had announced he would not return to the team for the 1979

season. The door had just swung wide open for Dale. It wasn't much afterward that Osterlund asked Dale if he wanted to be the team's primary driver for the 1979 season. Perhaps sensing what a talent he had in his midst, Osterlund wasn't about to let him get away.

"Man, I couldn't believe it," Dale later recalled. "I was going Winston Cup racing, and I didn't have to worry about paying for tires or engines or beating out dents in the fenders no more. The dream I'd had ever since I was a boy was coming true. It was like my daddy had told me once, 'If you work hard enough, your dream will come true.'"

Off and running

Dale's dream had come true. He entered 1979 poised for his first full season on the NASCAR circuit — a lifelong ambition fulfilled.

But, as one might expect with Dale, it was not enough. True, he had reached his goal. He was a full-time driver on the NASCAR circuit. But now he was determined to be the best.

Racing in a flashy blue and yellow car sponsored by Wrangler (The Jeans Machine), Dale was determined to make his mark.

The year got off to a rather inauspicious start for Dale, however, at the season's first race in Riverside, California, where he finished near the middle of the pack. But he opened some eyes with his next performance at the Daytona 500, where he scored a top-10 finish (No. 8) in just his second race as Osterlund's full-time driver. Dale continued to build on his impressive list of finishes, recording another top-10 finish at the North Wilkesboro Speedway.

His next challenge was the Southeastern 500, held on April Fool's Day in 1979. Dale's early performance through the first third of the season had already established that his rookie season was not to be taken lightly.

Not only was he competitive with racing's top drivers during his rookie campaign, Dale was among the Winston Cup leaders on the first of April — a ➔

Marcis, an early teammate of Dale's, greets Brett Bodine (right) in the garage at Talladega Speedway.

AP/WIDE WORLD PHOTOS

The Man in Black

contender for the points championship. Dale's qualifying lap placed him in ninth to start the race at the famed Bristol International Speedway, but by the time the April Fool's Day race was over, the joke was on Dale's competitors.

Earnhardt, at 28 years old and in just his 16th career Winston Cup series start, crossed the finish line first after leading for more than 160 laps and besting runner-up Bobby Allison by three seconds.

"I'll probably believe it in the morning," an ecstatic Earnhardt said after the race, according to Moriarty's biography. "This is a bigger thrill than my first-ever racing victory. This win was in the big leagues. It was against top-caliber drivers. It wasn't some dirt track back home."

Dale's success continued to grow surprisingly quickly, with more top-10 finishes coming as spring gave way to summer. And he continued to shock racing fans by hovering around the top of the Winston Cup points standings.

But on July 30, things would change. Leading nearly 100 laps into the Pocono 500, Dale suffered a horrific crash after one of his tires failed while negotiating the track's second turn. Dale was rushed to the hospital, where he found out he had broken both collar bones and suffered a concussion. His doctors told him he would be out of action for at least six-to-eight weeks.

"I was hurt in a lot of places, but the broken bones and the concussion and the headaches did not hurt as much as the frustration," Dale said. "I was worried that [Osterlund backup driver David] Pearson might do so well in that car that Osterlund would keep him and let me go." ➜

This 1982 crash at Pocono resulted in a mangled car and leg for Dale.

The Man in Black

And, in fact, Pearson did perform quite admirably in Dale's absence — even winning the Southern 500 in September. But Dale's spot was secure, and he returned to the track a week after the Southern 500 and went on to record seven additional top-10 performances before the end of the season. Although the Southeastern 500 would turn out to be Dale's only win in 1979, the season was a rousing success. Not just for a rookie, but for any driver.

Dale finished seventh in the Winston Cup points standings, complete with 11 top-five and 17 top-10 finishes. He owned four pole victories and amassed winnings of $264,085. Dale was the first rookie ever selected to compete in the International Race of Champions series.

Few then, were surprised when Dale was awarded the 1979 NASCAR Winston Cup Series Rookie of the Year Award. His accomplishments that year were impressive, to be sure.

"When I first started out, I worried about making it from week to week," he said after the race. "I worried about ever owning my own home. Now I've got a nice place on the lake. I am comfortable and I am building security."

Not a bad place to be, for a rookie. And, had his injury not sidelined him for nearly two months, there's no telling what more Dale my have been able to accomplish. Perhaps a Winston Cup title to go along with his Rookie of the Year Award? As it turns out, the title would come soon enough.

The legend is born

As we now know, Dale's Rookie of the Year performance in 1979 was just the opening scene in what would become one of the most successful acts in all of professional sports. The following season turned out to be even kinder to Dale. He followed up is 1979 Rookie of the Year award with yet another remarkable feat — the 1980 Winston Cup points championship. It would be the first of seven for Dale, tying the record set by "The King" Richard Petty.

But Dale's impressive run in 1979-80 was interrupted by some unexpected turmoil. He was surprised and hurt in 1981 when Osterlund stunned the racing world by selling his team to J.D. Stacy. Unhappy with the change of ownership, Dale abruptly left the team. But that upheaval would set the stage for one of racing's most formidable teams.

Dale would go on to team up with Richard Childress, a well-seasoned NASCAR racer whose ambition was to build a competitive team on the Winston Cup circuit. Although an experienced driver, Childress had achieved only marginal success in his years on the track — six top-five finishes.

Upon hearing that Dale was available, Childress seized his opportunity. He retired from racing and hired Earnhardt as his team's primary driver, and the foundation for success was quickly and firmly in place. Dale would reward the Childress racing team with six more Winston Cup points championships, although the next wouldn't come until six years later, when Dale edged out heated rival Darrell Waltrip.

But Dale's legend continued to grow and grow during those six years between his first two titles. He was a famously aggressive driver, never afraid to make

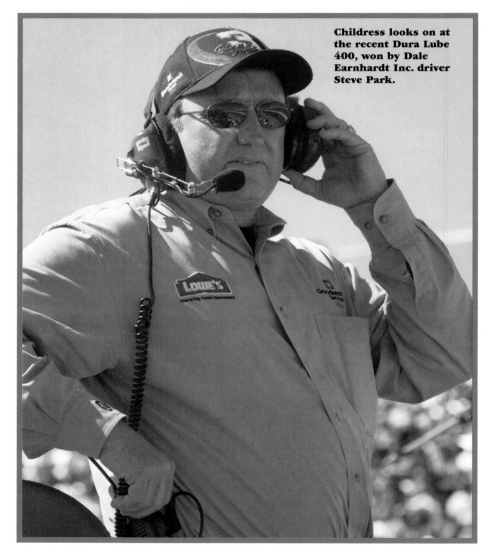

Childress looks on at the recent Dura Lube 400, won by Dale Earnhardt Inc. driver Steve Park.

contact or 'nudge' another driver out of his way. Of course, his aggressive approach was controversial, but that only helped feed the legend. He earned the nickname "The Intimidator," which seemed to be partly based on truth, and partly based on myth.

Fans either loved him or hated him. Either way Dale attracted an unparalleled amount of attention to his sport — and to himself, becoming one of the most widely recognized figures in all of sports.

Dale continued to dominate the racing circuit like few before him dared, including four points championships in five years ('90, '91, '93 and '94). And even when it appeared he had begun to lose his touch,' Dale responded with a flair that only he was capable of.

Saddled with a career-long winless streak of 59 races that lasted into the 1998 season, Dale broke out of his slump by winning the one race that vexed him through all of his years of racing. In his 22 years on the NASCAR circuit, Dale had never been able to win the Daytona 500.

But in 1998, just when the whispers began that "The Intimidator" had begun to falter, Dale broke through for a dramatic win in "America's Biggest Race." Dale had made no secret about his desire to win the Daytona 500, and his triumph in 1998 seemed to reinvigorate his career over the next three years.

But Dale's legacy doesn't end with him. Dale Jr. has already burst onto the NASCAR scene in nearly as dramatic and successful a fashion as his father did 22 years ago. Dale Jr. now races for the racing team his father built: Dale Earnhardt Inc.

Dale Earnhardt Sr. leaves behind a charisma and a record of success that will likely never be duplicated. His impressive career numbers speak to that. But when Dale is remembered in his proper place in history, he will be treasured for far greater achievements than just his numbers.

NASCAR's No. 3 — The Intimidator — will be remembered for much, much more than that. ■

Dale boasts the hardware he took at the 1988 Busch Clash.